CRIME AND RELIGIOUS BELIEFS IN INDIA

Kali, the Dreaded Goddess of Destruction.

From the original painting published by the Ravi-Varma Press, Bombay.

CRIME AND RELIGIOUS BELIEFS IN INDIA

AUGUSTUS SOMERVILLE

"AS A MAN THINKETH, SO IS HE"

GYAN

Published by

GYAN

Gyan Publishing House
5, Ansari Road
Daryaganj, New Delhi-110002
Phone: 011-47034999, 9811692060
E-mail: books@gyanbooks.com

Distribution Network
gyanbooks.com
India, USA, Canada, UK, Australia, France

ISBN : 9788121232777 (PB)
First Published, Jaffina, 1905

2nd Impression 2020

Printed at: Gyan Press, Delhi.

Crime and Religious Beliefs in India
Author: Augustus Somerville

CRIME AND RELIGIOUS BELIEFS IN INDIA.

By

AUGUSTUS SOMERVILLE

Author of

"Shikar near Calcutta," "A Guide to Darjeeling," etc.

—:o:—

"As a man thinketh, so is he."

"The Criminologist"

CALCUTTA,

1931.

To

Lt.-Col. W. G. HAMILTON, I.M.S.,

(Late) Inspector-General of Prisons, Bengal.

This Book is

Respectfully Dedicated.

CONTENTS.

INTRODUCTION.

To understand the mentality of the Indian, it is essential to have first an insight into some of the more important social and religious customs in this country. It is no exaggeration to say that the average Indian "lives and moves and has his being" in an atmosphere pregnant with religious beliefs and superstitions.

From early infancy his mind is trained in strictly religious channels. On every hand he sees manifestation of the divine. He is steeped in the complicated mythology of his race and learns early to attribute every event of his social and domestic life to religious influences. Ignorant and deeply religious he is prone to accept, unquestioned, superstitions and folk-tales of the most grotesque kind. His religious susceptibilities make him an easy victim for wandering mendicants. Yogis, Fakirs and the like prey on his good nature, his dread of the unknown and on the characteristic hospitality of his race. In perfect good faith, and all unconscious of its incongruity, he will pray devotedly in the morning to some tutelary deity for the success of his crops, and that very evening will ask a divine blessing on the *dacoity* he is about to commit.

Crime in India may be said to originate from three main sources. Religious controversies and practices, women, and land disputes. The first two are the most prolific factors in crime affecting the person. To it may be traced the majority of murders, dacoities and assaults that fill our police records; while to the third our Civil Courts probably owe their existence.

In this little book I have made a very modest attempt to demonstrate some of the more apparent and interesting features of crime that shew a distinct bearing on the influence of religious beliefs and customs. I have avoided details. It is extraordinary what dull reading, anything like a detailed account of crime and criminal methods in this country would provide. The East has none of the sensationalism of the West, but for skill and ingenuity I doubt if we can be beaten.

I have dealt with prostitution and the "dope" traffic, but here also, the reader must readjust his outlook. Prostitution in India must be viewed from a different standpoint to that which we are accustomed. Prostitutes are treated with a degree of respect, are tolerated and even encouraged in India, to an extent incomprehensible to Western standards of ethical thought. Sanctified harlotry is a *fait accompli* and is an institution as old as India itself.

Understanding some of the difficulties that will beset the casual reader I have so arranged my subject that by first giving him an insight into the religious customs of the people, their folk-tales and superstitions, I lead him to grasp some of the significance of human sacrifice, the casting of helpless infants to sacred crocodiles, and the various other atrocities that we call crime, but which, to the ignorant villager, is but the performance of a sacred duty.

It will be observed that I have used Calcutta as a sort of background for my descriptions of night haunts, opium dens, gambling saloons and the like. I have done this principally because I am best acquainted with the underworld of this city, but the description given would apply with few modifications to similar resorts in any other large city in India.

The subject of crime, in spite of its vast human appeal, is a subject in which the average man seldom takes any interest, and books on crime suffer the well-known fate of Blue Books; which are relegated to the book-shelf and there lost and forgotten.

In order to save this book from a similar fate, I have hit upon the expedient of presenting my subject in narrative form. Such a medium makes it at once interesting and readable but does not in any way detract from its value as a treatise on one of the many aspects of crime. This will explain what would otherwise prove a jarring element in a serious work of this type,—humorous incidents, folk tales and imaginary sketches—these are all the trappings, the real, genuine worth lies within.

Further, I am no evangelist but I do honestly believe, that a little more Christian fortitude and forbearance on both sides, a little more love and a spirit of intellectual brotherhood, would do much to mitigate many of the evils, religious, social and domestic, that mar to this day, the homely, inoffensive lives of good and honest men in this beautiful "Land of Ind."

I am indebted to the editors of the "Times of India, Illustrated Weekly," Bombay and of the "Illustrated Pioneer Mail," Allahabad, for their kind courtesy in permitting me to reproduce such parts of this book as have already appeared in their esteemed journals. My thanks are also due to Mr. S. M. Edwardes, C. S. I., C. V. O., from whose excellent little volume, "Crime in India," I have culled much that is of historical interest regarding prostitution in this country.

To Lt. Col. W. G. Hamilton, I. M. S., Inspector-General of Prisons, Bengal, who has done me the great courtesy of permitting me to dedicate this book to him, I am very grateful for the kind encouragement he has given me in the preparation of this volume.

In conclusion, I desire to acknowledge my indebtedness to the proprietors of the "Statesman" for the valuable press reports that have been incorporated in this book.

Calcutta.
21st May, 1929.

Augustus Somerville.

PREFACE TO SECOND EDITION.

I am glad of the opportunity the publication of this revised edition offers to remove certain misconceptions that have arisen regarding the original intention of this book.

I admit that the selection of a title such as "Crime and Religious Beliefs in India" is open both to ambiguity and misunderstanding. Religion has no bearing on crime. Theoretically this is correct but actually history offers no single parallel so prone to provoke the worst of human passion as religious intolerance. There is no worthy emotion, belief or desire in the heart of man that through ignorance, misconception or deliberate intention is not capable of evil and so it is with those deeply psychological oriental beliefs, so pure at their source, yet so much maligned and distorted by ignorance and prejudice by the common mass. It is my intention in this book to shew the influence of these customs and beliefs on certain sections of crime in this country. Man reacts subconsciously to his environment and his religious beliefs influenced his moral and social outlook. Bearing this in mind the reader will have no difficulty in following my idea of first describing certain religious customs and then enumerating crimes that have a direct bearing on these. Mind you, I write of the ignorant masses only, no cultured, educated Indian would for a moment tolerate such superstitions.

Another thing. Many of the sites mentioned

in this book have now ceased to exist. When this volume was first conceived and written the Calcutta Improvement Trust had not started its activities and congested areas in the heart of the city flourished in all their pristine squalor and filth. Since then light and cleanliness has descended like a mantle on this "Packed and pestilential town" and Bentinck Street, such as we knew it, has ceased to exist. Chore Hat has been renovated—a new second-hand market having sprung up at the Sealdah end of Bow Bazar. Karaya, with its unenviable reputation has been swept clean and now emerges under the more euphonious title of Park Circus while even the congested areas in the Indian quarter have all responded to a more enlightened and hyginic civic administration. To those who wish to see Calcutta as it used to be I would recommend a perusal of "Thacker's Guide to Calcutta" by the Rev. W. G. Firminger, M.A.

In conclusion, I should like once again to acknowledge my indebtedness to those papers that have permitted me to incorporate their valuable press reports on criminal cases. In particular to the "Statesman," "Amrit Bazar Patrika," and "Liberty."

Calcutta.
October, 22nd. 1930.

Augustus Somerville.

CRIME AND RELIGIOUS BELIEFS IN INDIA.

CHAPTER I.

PROSTITUTION.

IN dealing with Prostitution in India I have divided the subject into three divisions or aspects, namely: Historical, Religious and Modern.

The subject is an unpleasant one to write on but in a work such as this it forms a *sine qua non.* It is the root cause, the source and mainstay of our brothels, opium dens and gambling saloons. Without prostitution the revenue earned by these dens of iniquity would soon cease. The sexual element predominates in all such haunts of vice and crime and is such a fruitful source of income that I doubt if there is a single "Night Haunt" in Calcutta which does not harbour a few of these unfortunate women to cater to their regular customers, or, by singing and dancing, attract fresh trade.

Eastern prostitution differs materially from the western or rather European. In India prostitution is tolerated, in fact, encouraged to an extent that finds no counterpart in European countries. There is reason for this.

A HISTORICAL REVIEW.

The profession of harlotry in India is sanctified by both Time and Tradition. It is mentioned in the Rig Veda and the Buddhist Jatakas, which were written about 359-300 B. C., that courtesans were not only encouraged, but commanded a certain amount of respect. They were accommodated in the royal palaces, were highly paid and occupied a recognized position in the social scale. They even acquired a certain legendary distinction: Ambapali, the famous hetaera of Visala, figures in Buddhist legend, while the Princess Salavati adopted the prostitute's calling to further her own aims.

In addition to this we learn from the "Arthasastra" compiled by Kautilya, Chandragupta's Brahman minister, that during the Mauryan Empire (325-298 B. C.) prostitutes occupied a well defined position in the Royal Court. Their duties were principally those of bathroom servants, shampooers, bedroom attendants, washerwomen and garland-makers. They waited upon the King, presented him with water, scents, fragrant powders, flowers etc., and were supervised and controlled by an official known as "The Superintendent of Prostitutes." From among the more beautiful and accomplished were selected those who were privileged to hold the royal umbrella, fan the King and accompany him on his travels. They were generally trained in singing and dancing and were from the very nature of their calling expected to earn their up-keep by selling their favours to all comers. That their daily earnings amounted to a considerable sum is not unlikely, for the Mauryan Government appears to have levied on each prostitute attached to the Royal Household a tax amounting to two days' earnings per month or an equivalent of 7 per cent. of her total monthly income and to secure for the State so profitable a source of revenue made it a criminal offence for these women to marry or to refuse their favours to any man willing to pay for them, the offence being punishable with a flogging or a fine and in extreme cases death by burning or drowning. Coming to the early centuries of the Christian Era (200 B. C.— A. D. 200) we find from the "Institutes of Manu," the moral textbook of the orthodox Hindu, and from the "Kama Sutra" of Satsyayana written about A. D. 250-300, that prostitutes then also occupied a recognized position in the social and political life of the nation. Their calling, far from being despised, was looked up to with a certain degree of respect and was adopted by women as an honourable profession, much as Nursing or Midwifery is adopted to-day by women of all grades and classes.

RELIGIOUS BELIEFS AND CUSTOMS.

Sanctified harlotry is in vogue all over India, even to the present day. It is a survival of the old Dravidian form of worship and its origin is obvious. The worship of earth-mothers and the conception of nature in the birth of the seasons; the folk-lore of the agricultural sections of the people who believe that the fertility of the soil depends on the periodical marriage of the earth-goddess with a male consort—usually rain,—has found its natural expression in sacred prostitutes whose duties are to serve the Gods and to reproduce in their own lives, as closely as possible, the various amours of the goddesses they impersonate.

Besides serving in the Temples these women have certain privileges or powers attributed to them. They are looked upon as bearers of good luck, particularly at marriage feasts, where their presence confers special blessings on the Bride. As she can never become a widow a prostitute is often deputed to walk at the head of Hindu marriage processions. Her "Tali" (neck ornament) is specially regarded as a most potent talisman and many Hindus send the "Tali" required for the forthcoming bride to one of these sacred prostitutes who prepares the string for it and threads it with beads from her own necklet.

Some idea of the strange mentality of the Hindu and his ideas on prostitution may be gathered from the fact that even the Brahmin priest considers the very dust at the door of a prostitute's house to be holy. To the Brahmin licentiousness in any form is a crime and the man who visits a prostitute so debases himself that he sheds every virtue he possesses on her very threshold. Hence the dust here is holy and on certain days this dust is collected and laid before the idol as an offering.

MODERN WHITE-SLAVE TRAFFIC—AND A TALE

With regard to the White-Slave Traffic, Arab, Jew, and Indian agents have so far commercialized this profession that it is rapidly losing the hold upon the imagination of the people it once had. The Indian term "Rundee" applied to all classes of prostitutes is a term of contempt. The calling itself has fallen into disrepute so that only the lowest classes and those forced to adopt this profession as a last resource are now to be found among these unfortunates.

Certain criminal tribes of course still adopt this profession as a regular means of income, but these do not influence the position in large cities.

The system of recruitment, however, still exists as a menace to society and the ways of the Trafficker make interesting reading. The following press account from the "Statesman" of 6th November 1928 gives some idea of the extent to which this abhorrent trade is prevalent in the United Provinces and the difficulties with which the police have to contend when bringing these "White Slave" traffickers to book:

"The police of the United Provinces have started a fresh and particularly active campaign against traffickers in women, for criminals of this character, I have been reliably informed, are increasing, despite stringent measures, including severe sentences in court, to suppress them.

"Numerous and varied are the methods adopted by these criminals and the police realize that they are faced with a very difficult problem.

"What makes their task all the more formidable is the fact that the activities of the traffickers in women cover a wide area. Though their business begins in the United Provinces where the female population preponderates over that of the male, it has its ramifications in the Punjab, the North West Frontier Province, Sind, the Central Provinces, Bengal and even in Nepal.

"Moreover, it is known that the criminals include all castes and classes, from the Pathan and the Punjabi Mussulman to the Hindus of the United Provinces and the Central Provinces as well as the Nepalese.

"Nepalese girls are reputed to be beautiful and they find a ready sale in the plains of India.

"An example of this fact is a case which has just come to public notice at Lucknow. Two women acted as decoys. They were Nepalese and selected as their victim a girl named Amu living in the little village of Tal Pokaranj, in the district of Peuthan (Nepal).

"They started by cultivating the acquaintance of Amu's parents and flattered the girl herself, who was only ten years of age, by telling her that she would easily find a rich husband were she to go to India. So successfully did they ingratiate themselves into the confidence of Amu's people that the mother and father were easily induced to allow their daughter to accompany the two women to a fair which was to take place somewhere in India.

"That was seven months ago and since then, needless to say, the parents have never heard of their little daughter. The two women, it has now been revealed, took the girl to Lucknow where they kept her closely confined. The manner of her subsequent escape reads like a story book romance.

"Sitting alone in her room one night Amu overheard her captors engaged in conversation, and to her horror she heard them decide to send her to Calcutta where she was to be sold. At the first opportunity she ran out of the house and fortunately came across a Nepalese from her own native village. The police were soon informed and Amu will shortly be returning to her parents.

"Amu's experience is almost identical with that of other girls who happen to fall victims to cunning harpies. But where she was fortunate in her escape many hundreds of others are subjected to a much worse fate.

"Among these are often girls from the United Provinces who, owing to the proportionately smaller male population, find difficulty in getting married. These girls fall an easy prey to the wiles of kidnappers who, the police are aware, form themselves into gangs in large towns. These gangs employ women to procure girls for them to sell and give them extremely high wages for their trouble.

"The police have also been able to discover the chief centres from which these gangs operate. These are:—

In the United Provinces.—Mirzapur, Lucknow, Benares, Cawnpore, Agra and Allahabad.

In the Punjab.—Amritsar, Lahore, Rawalpindi and Delhi.

In the N.-W. F. Province.—Peshawar.

"One of the largest of these gangs has its headquarters at Mirzapur and at Amritsar, its chief business being conducted in the two provinces in which those towns are situated. These two places have been selected with a purpose. It is well known that they are large carpet-manufacturing centres. The gang has devised the ingenious scheme of dealing, not in girls, but in "carpets." Thus, when a sufficiently large number of girls have been decoyed to the gang's houses of confinement in Mirzapur, a telegram reaches the head of the gang in Amritsar telling him that three or four, as the case may be, "carpets" are being sent with a certain person by a particular train on a given date. The Amritsar people understand and the "carpets" are taken over when they arrive and distributed in due course to various places in the Punjab.

"The gang has another method to distinguish between the qualities and attractions of the girls they traffic in. "Carpets" being the commodity of their trade, they describe in their telegrams beautiful and well-favoured girls, who will be sold for as much as Rs. 10,000 as "red carpets." Girls who are not so well-favoured in the matter of looks are known as "blue carpets"; and others, who generally find their way into houses of ill-fame, are known as "black carpets."

"Another case came to light recently in a most remarkable manner.

"A constable on duty at the Lahore Railway Station was surprised to hear a woman's voice crying out from a third-class compartment of a train which had just drawn up,—"I have been kidnapped. Rescue me!"

"The policeman took the woman off the train, whereupon she related a surprising story. She said that three days previously she had been sold by two men and two women at Amritsar to a man then in the compartment for Rs. 650. Originally, she said, she had come from Lucknow. She pointed out the man on the train who, she said, had bought her. This man was arrested, but he said that he had bought the girl to marry her and had no intention of selling her."

I have often questioned these unfortunate women as to how they were first induced to adopt this degrading profession. The stories told are more or less typical. There is usually a tale of deception; of false marriages or of economic stress. I however recount a tale which will serve as an example of the peculiar danger to which young and inexperienced girls are subjected to in this country, and one which may well serve as a warning.

In one of the better class houses in Karaya, a quarter set apart for European prostitutes, I once came across a young woman of about twenty-five. From her conversation I gathered that she had been well educated. Her manners were refined and the terms in which she spoke of her present occupation and the men who visited her convinced me that the girl was thoroughly disgusted with her mode of life and anxious to escape—*if she could.* Let me tell her story.

Born of genteel parents in London, the girl was well educated and later trained as a nursery gover-

2

ness. About four years prior to my having met her, she saw an advertisement in the "Daily Mail" requiring the services of a nursery governess to look after the three children of a certain well known Divine, at that time serving as Pastor of a small parish near Calcutta. The salary offered and the conditions of service were good and she applied for the post, receiving in reply a very nice letter from the Pastor and her passage money in advance. She arrived in India early in January and took up her duties immediately, serving the Pastor for nearly three years before the incidents I am about to narrate befell.

It is a peculiar characteristic of most European people that they seldom recognize the limit at which kindness to a menial ceases and familiarity begins. The women-folk are the greatest offenders in this respect and it is strange that they alone are unconscious of the fact that the servant they treat with such exemplary kindness has long ceased to have any respect for them. The case I describe is a typical instance of how such familiarity usually ends. Home-trained, home-bred, unconscious of the emotions she was stirring or the evil passions she was arousing, the young nurse, in her daily round of duties, her long walks with the children, morning and evening, failed to detect in the young Mohammedan Bearer whose duty it was to accompany and assist her the first signs of suppressed desire. What followed I give in her own words.

"Returning home late one evening, we took a short cut through a lonely field. Here the bearer, who was carrying one of the children, suddenly set the child down and coming up to me caught hold of my hand, endeavouring to kiss it. Disgusted and alarmed, I ordered the man to let my hand go immediately and as he still persisted I struck him sharply across the face. The blow had the desired effect. The man released my hand and on his knees begged of me to forgive him and not to mention the incident to the Pastor, who would surely dismiss him. Against my better judgment I consented and the matter apparently ended there. But I was yet to learn something of the subtleties of the Eastern mind and the extent to which such brutes will go to gain their ends. One Sunday as I was resting in my room after dressing the children for Sunday school I heard a knock at my door and the same bearer entered with a plate of Indian sweetmeats which he laid on the table near my bed intimating that it was a peace offering and a token of his sorrow for his past rudeness. I accepted the offering in the spirit in which it was given and later, when he had left the room, ate a few which I found delicious. From that moment I was a lost woman. Whatever drug those sweets contained, they acted swiftly and effectively. I became like a woman possessed. Every vestige of maidenly decency left me. Pleading a bad headace I kept my room. In vain I strove to master myself. The Pastor and his family were away at church and I was alone in the house. Shortly after they left the bearer came to my room. Maddened by the drug, resistance was useless and with him I fled to a low brothel in the heart of the Bazar where I was subjected to every brutality his lust could invent.

Not satisfied with outraging me himself, he brought his friends and his friends their friends. They plied me with food and drink, all of which must have been drugged in the same way, for after a while I lost all consciousness of what I did or where I went, till I was rescued by the police and taken to hospital. Here, I gradually came back to a normal consciousness and a true appreciation of the awful extent of my shame. My subsequent history is too familiar to bear repetition. It is the one tale of all fallen women. I drifted lower and lower till I took to prostitution as a last resource."

I will not comment on the sory this woman told—it needs none; but the moral is obvious.

CHAPTER II.

DEVADASIS.

A subject that has aroused considerable interest recently and has given rise to no little controversy, mostly of an acrimonius nature, has been that ancient custom whereby young girls are dedicated to Hindu temples. These women are known as Devadasis or to put it more crudely, Sacred Prostitutes.

As explained in the previous chapter, sanctified harlotry has been in vogue in India for a considerable time and the Devadasi is the natural outcome. Originally the conception of a Devadasi was a long way removed from the poor harlot of present times. History offers a parallel in the Vestal Virgin; the Nun and those noble women who sacrificed wealth, power and position to dedicate their lives to the particular deity they worshipped. As to the duties and position of the Devadasi originally, the following extract from Lajpat Rai's book, "Unhappy India" should prove interesting.

"In India the dancing girls dedicated to the service of the Tamil temples take the name of devadasis 'servants of the gods' but in common parlance they are spoken of simply as harlots. Every Tamil temple of note in Southern India has its troop of these sacred women. Their official duties are to dance twice a day morning and evening, in the temple, to fan the idol with Tibetan ox-tails, to dance and sing before it when it is borne in procession and to carry the holy light called Kumbarti. In order to obtain a safe delivery expectant mothers will often vow to dedicate their child if she should prove to be a girl to the service of god. Among the weavers of Tirukullikundram a little town in the Madras Presidency the eldest daughter of every family is devoted to the temple. Girls thus made over to the deity are formally married, sometimes to the idol, sometimes to a sword, before they enter on their duties; from which it appears that they are often if not regularly regarded as the wives of the god."

"Among the Kaikolans, a large caste of Tamil weavers who are spread all over Southern India at least one girl in every family should be dedicated to the temple service. The ritual, as it is observed at the initiation of one of these girls in Coimbatore, includes a form of nuptial ceremony."

"In Travancore a dancing girl attached to a temple is known as a 'servant of god'. The following account of her dedication and way of life deserves to be quoted because while it ignores the baser side of her vocation it brings clearly out the idea of her marriage to the deity. Marriage in the case of a Devaratial in its original import is a renunciation of ordinary family life and a consecration to the service of god. With a lady nurse at a hospital or a sister at a Convent a

Devadasi at a Hindu shrine, such as she probably was in the early ages of Hindu spirituality would have claimed favourable comparison. In the ceremonial of the dedication—marriage of the dasi, elements are not wanting which indicate a past quite the reverse of disreputable. The girl to be married is generally from six to eight years in age. The bridegroom is the presiding deity in the local temple. Thenceforth she becomes the wife of the deity in the sense that she formally and solemnly dedicates the rest of her life to his service with the same constancy and devotion that a faithful wife united in holy matrimony shows to her wedded lord. The life of a Devadasi bedecked with all the accomplishments that the muses could give was one of spotless purity. Even now she is maintained by the temple. She undertakes fasts in connection with the temple festivals, such as the seven days' fast for the Apamaragam ceremony. During the period of this fast, strict continence is enjoined; she is required to take only one meal, and that within the temple—in fact to live and behave at least for a term in the manner ordained for her throughout life. Some of her daily work seems interesting; she attends the Diparadhana, the waving of lighted lamps in front of deity at sunset every day, sings hymns in his praise, dances before his presence and goes round with him in processions with lights in hand. After the procession, she sings a song or two from Jayadeva's Gitagovinda and with a few lullaby hymns her work for the night is over. When she grows physically unfit for these duties she is formally invalidated by a special ceremony, i.e., Totuvaikkuwa (old mother) and is entitled only to a subsistence allowance. When she dies, the temple contributes to the funeral expenses. On her deathbed the priest attends and after a few ceremonies immediately after death, gets her bathed with saffron-powder."

From the above it will be seen that the original conception of this calling was not the ignoble institution it is to-day. That it exists and is practiced in all the large temples in India here is no question of doubt, but in some districts, this unfortunate custom is more prevalent than in others. In Madras particularly, the seat of Brahmanism in its worst aspects, we find the Devadasi in her most degraded form. So much in this institution resented by the more enlightened people of this province, that Mrs. S. Muthulakshmi Reddi has recently introduced a Bill in the Madras Legislative Council for its abolition. As this Bill throws much light on the subject, I reproduce it in full.

BILL NO. 5 OF 1930.

A Bill to prevent the dedication of women to Hindu temples in the Presidency of Madras.

Whereas the dedication of women to Hindu temples results in such women adopting the profession of prostitute dancing girls, it is desirable and expedient to put an end to the practice of such dedication — Preamble.

and whereas the previous sanction of the Governor-General in Council has been obtained; It is enacted as follows:—

Short title.

1. This Act shall be called "The Prevention of Dedication Act, 1930."

Dedication of Hindu women to temples declared Illegal.

2. The performance in the precincts of Hindu temples or other places of worship of *pottukattu* or *gajje puja* or any similar ceremony to a Hindu woman with a view to dedicate her is hereby declared illegal and shall be illegal.

Dedicated women may contract valid marriages.

3. A Hindu woman who has gone through a process of dedication by the performance of *pottukattu* or *gajje puja* or any similar ceremony may thereafter contract a legal marriage and it shall be recognized as valid notwithstanding any law or custom to the contrary.

Penalty for dedication of women to temples.

4. Whoever permits, performs or takes part in the performance or abets the performance within the precincts of a Hindu temple of the ceremony of *pottukatu* or *gajje puja* or any similar ceremony with a view to dedicate any Hindu woman shall be punished with imprisonment of either description for a term which may extend to one year and shall also be liable to fine.

5. Nothing in this Act shall be construed to prevent any person from being liable under section 372 of the Indian Penal Code or under any other law to any other or higher punishment than is provided by this Act; provided that no person shall be prosecuted under this Act, if he was convicted under any of the provisions of law mentioned above.

Saving of penalty provided by other law.

STATEMENT OF OBJECTS AND REASONS.

"Not only the inam-holding devadasis but also other devadasis dedicate a large number of girls to Hindu temples by going through pottukattu or gajje puja or similar ceremony in Hindu temples. Whatever the origin of the practice in ancient days of the dedication of women as devadasis in Hindu temples, it is unfortunately the case that the practice has now degenerated mainly into a method of initiation of young women to a life of immorality and prostitution. The existence or otherwise of shastraic sanction to the practice of dedication as devadasis is therefore immaterial. The shastras are against vice and impurity of all kinds, and enlightened public opinion is against tolerating the continuance of a practice which, in the name of service to God, has condemned a certain class of women to a life of either concubinage or prostitution. A Hindu woman who is so dedicated is considered by custom to be incapable of contracting a valid marriage thereafter. Therefore, it is highly desirable and expedient to prohibit the performance of dedication of girls to Hindu temples within the precincts of any temples and legalise the marriage of such girls when contracted after such dedication. There have been previous attempts at putting an end to this practice of dedication, but they have been, so to say, indirect and have not produced the desired result. By amendments to sections 372 and 373 of the Indian Penal Code, the age-limit for the disposal of minor girls for purposes of prostitution has been raised from 16 to 18 years. But though at the time when this change was effected it was supposed that it would reduce, if not put an end to, the evil of dedication of girls to temples, it has failed to achieve this result, because it does not deal with the dedication of girls as a whole. Sections 372 and 373 of the Indian Penal Code are evaded by the temples allowing dedication after the girl attains 18 years of age; and in the moffusal even minor girls are dedicated even to-day, because the temple authorities, the parent and the general public honestly feel that religion sanctions it and the law is not absolutely against it.

"A legislative enactment is therefore necessary in this province for dealing with the practice of dedication *per se* of Hindu girls and women without touching the existing penalties for the disposal of minor girls for immoral purposes dealt with by sections 372 and 373 of the Indian Penal Code.

" My object in bringing in this Bill is twofold: firstly, to have a law declaring that dedicating of girls to Hindu temples is illegal and to prohibit such dedication; and secondly, to punish the persons taking part in the ceremony of dedication. In this connexion I may point out that in the adjoining Indian State of Mysore, the Government have prohibited the dedication of girls in Muzrai temples. The Mysore Government prohibited the dedication of Hindu girls in its temples by proceedings dated 28th January 1910, which runs thus: "The Government observe that whatever may be the euphemism by which the true nature of the ceremony is concealed, *Gajje puja* has an intimate connexion with dedication to the profession of a prostitute dancing girl. They are not prepared to allow the performance of such a ceremony in a Muzrai temple, and are satisfied from depositions and the opinion of the Muzrai Agamik on record that no hardship will be caused by the prohibition of the performance of such ceremonies in temples.

They accordingly prohibit the performance of Gajje puja or any similar ceremony within the precincts of any temple under the control of Government in the Muzrai department."

"If the British Government in India have not yet undertaken legislation on the point, it is probably out of a tender regard to alleged religious susceptibilities of Hindus. To show that public opinion is in favour of the abolition of the system, and in response to the appeal of several men and women associations and hundreds of enlightened members of the community of devadasis themselves, I have brought forward this Bill."

Following my intention of describing how certain religious beliefs and customs influence the minds of the ignorant masses, I will now turn to a subject which I consider is the natural outcome of a mentality that accepts unquestioned an institution in which harlotry plays an important role in sacerdotal affairs.

OUTRAGES ON WOMEN.

This is a subject, which in recent years, has attracted the attention and stirred the public imagination to such an extent, that local journals, both Indian and European, have voiced their indignation in no uncertain terms.

Recently the "Amrita Bazar Patrika" a daily that caters for a large section of the more educated Indian public took up the instance of the "Sovana Abduction Case." The following is a brief history of the case as reported by that paper:—

"Accepting the verdict of jury who by a majority of 3 to 2 found accused Mahiuddin guilty under Sections 376 I. P. C. (Rape) and 366 (kidnapping) for abducting Sovana Ray, the fourteen year minor daughter of Charu Ray, Pleader, Mr. Stork, District and Sessions Judge sentenced the accused to undergo rigorous imprisonment for two years. The accused was further sentenced under Section 120B (conspiracy) to 18 months R. I. the sentences to run concurrently.

Hemayatuddin Mukhtear another accused was also found guilty under Sections 366 and 120B I. P. C. and sentenced to 18 months rigorous imprisonment.

The prosecution story was that about the 30th of April last the two accused conspired and agreed to kidnap Sovana Ray minor girl below 14 years of age from the care and protection of her father Babu Charu Chandra Ray. The girl was then taken away from her father's house by the first accused and kept at different and far off places like Vizagapatam and Bombay. On a warrant issued by the District Magistrate of Barisal the first accused was arrested at Bombay.

The girl deposed that when on the 30th April 1929, at night she was poked through a hole in the window ledge she got up and came out after opening the door. Mahiuddin joined her. An I. A. student also was there. They took her to the house of Gani constable. From here she was taken to the steamer by Khalek and Mohiuddin. Next day at 11 a. m. she, Mohiuddin, and Khalek got down at Chandpur. Khalek hired a *nouka.* In that *nouka* they went to the house of the Pisi of Khalek. The house is a pucca one. They had their meals there. At about 8 p.m. they left the place in two *noukas.* In one boat were the girl and Mohiuddin. In this boat Mohiuddin raped her. From Chandpur via Goalundo, Naihati, Bandel and Howrah they—Mohiuddin and the girl came to Balasore. From Balasore via Waltair they went to Vizagapatam. At Vizagapatam they lived for about a month in the rented house of Rezzak Mia. The girl deposed that at Vizagapatam they gave out that they were a married couple. Then they visited the house of a Bengalee gentleman who works in the Railway office. The girl deposes that accused Hemayat advised them through letter—to go further away as warrants had been issued for their arrest. On receipt of this letter they left Vizagapatam. They went to Hyderabad. After a few days stay at Hyderabad they came to Bombay. At Bombay they were arrested. Charu Babu brought the girl from Bombay."

The details of this case are sordid and commonplace enough to justify the average reader in dismissing the matter as a typical instance of abduction and rape. But this case fulfilled an important mission. It brought to light an amazing state of affairs, inasmuch as it showed the extent to which such cases were increasing in this country.

Mr. Justice Costello, who tried this case, made some scathing comments on the character of the the accused and added the following significant remarks:—

"It was intolerable that in a civilised community women should be liable to be outraged in this manner. If men could not control their passions, this court must take such steps as to make them do so. It should be distinctly understood that if this kind of offence continued to be prevalent stern measures would have to be adopted for suppressing it even by sentencing the offender to transportation for life."

Nor did the matter rest here. The "Amrita Bazar Patrika" devoted the major portion of a column to this case, and its observations, inspite of its racial bias, are obviously sincere in its endurance to impress on the public mind the need for stricter legislation, to suppress this growing evil. It comments as follows:—

"A correspondent has drawn our attention to the fact that in the printed list of criminal cases at the High Court for this session about ninety per cent of the cases are of the nature of kidnapping or abduction, that is, oppression on women. An examination of the Sessions cases in the Mofussil courts, we believe, will reveal the same state of affairs. We have times without number invited the attention of the Government to the prevalence of crimes of this nature. In the rural areas which are practically unprotected by the Police it is the hooligans who rule and their most favorite pastime is the kidnapping or abduction of women.

Mr. Justice Costello has given a plain hint to the Government to make the law more drastic than it is in the matter of crimes against women. It is not enough to make the punishment of such crimes more severe but the law should be amended in such a way that persons who by giving shelter or otherwise facilitate the commission of the crime or the escape of the offender may be brought within the operation of the law. It is a commonplace occurrence for kidnappers to take their victims from place to place and from house to house and the persons who thus give shelter are often allowed to escape prosecution either because of the corruption of the Police or the inadequacy of the law.

Mr. Justice Costello's remarks should not be lost on the courts of law in the mofussil. Many of the judges are disposed to be lenient in awarding punishments for such crimes. It is not permissible to pry into the inwardness of their mentality but the tendency is extremely regrettable. The lenient sentence in what is known as the Sovana abduction case is one among numerous instances of misplaced judicial leniency. Such punishments only encourage crimes of this description. The case was proved to the hilt and yet two of the jurors found the accused not guilty. We do not know what impelled these two jurymen to pronounce the verdict they did. It has however been manifest in numerous cases of this nature that some of the jurors are influenced by communal sympathy for the accused in their verdict. We think the least that should be done in such cases is to remove the names of such persons from the jury list and disqualify them for-ever from sitting as jurors. The immediate need of the hour is to undertake legislation and take effective executive action to suppress crimes of this nature."

I would leave this question as it stands were it not for one outstanding feature and that is the extraordinary simplicity and ignorance of the average Indian girl. In the case just mentioned the girl herself deposed that "she was poked through a hole in the window ledge, she got up and came out after opening the door." There is no mention that the girl raised an alarm, that she attempted to awaken her parents or even to resist the attempts at abduction. All she did was to follow quietly. Had such a case been put before an English jury the verdict would have been one of connivance. I will quote another instance:—

"Mr. Clifford Norohne, Deputy Magistrate of Howrah, had before him a case in which Khonda Pakray and a woman of the town named Biraji were prosecuted for kidnapping and concealing a minor girl for immoral purposes.

4

It was alleged that Panchi Dassi (12), the kidnapped girl, on the last Bhadra Sankranti day went to the Ghat in the early hour of the morning to have a bath. The first accused approached her and asked her to accompany him promising gift of some ornaments of which he is said to have made a show in her presence. She was taken to the house of Biraji, and thence to another house nearby where she was kept during the night and removed again to the house of Biraji on day break. The first accused is alleged to have had an illicit intercourse with the girl."

In this instance also (and I could cite such cases *ad nauseam*) the ease with which the girl is abducted, the extraordinary lack of any sense of self protection is an outstanding feature. The cause is not far to seek, but as I am dealing with crime and not social reform, I will leave this question to abler pens, still I feel that I would be neglecting a heaven sent opportunity if I failed to remind my Indian friends, who have voiced and upheld the perfection and beauty of Indian womanhood that India's future greatness lies in the emancipation of just such women as these; whose freedom rests not in the hands of missonaries and social reformers, but in the intelligent co-operation of their own kith and kin and whose education on broader and more liberal lines is as essential as that of the male and more favourably placed members of the family.

CHAPTER III.

"DOPE" TRAFFIC.

BEFORE actually dealing with the taking of drugs, the conducting of opium dens and the like, it will be interesting to learn how opium, cocaine, hashish, Indian hemp (colloquially known as "Ganja") and other drugs are smuggled out of and into the country. I am indebted to an old Custom House Officer, whose experiences in detecting cases of opium smuggling and the like extend over several years for the following details of the modus operandi of the opium and cocaine smuggler.

"From time to time reports appear in the press to the effect that the Customs Officers have seized a quantity of opium or cocaine aboard a certain ship. Sometimes an arrest is effected, but more often than not the "dope" alone is seized.

A mercantile marine officer who gets a billet on board a ship trading between Calcutta, China and Japan, is not on board very long before he runs up against the opium and cocaine traffic. Being a game of chance and adventure, it appeals as such to the average young man, quite apart from its financial possibilities, which are in themselves very tempting, for it is possible within the course of three or four years to acquire quite a modest fortune. On the other hand of course there is always the liability of being caught which means a penalty of anything up to three years' rigorous imprisonment, not to mention the loss of one's job.

If the " recruit " decides to take a hand in the smuggling game he is at the first opportunity made acquainted by his shipmates with the various sources of supply of opium in Calcutta, which are generally represented by Chinaman who import the drug from up-country at considerable risk of being detected by-Excise men. Usually the opium takes the form of hard black balls, about three inches in diameter and is smuggled into Calcutta by train.

In Calcutta if the seaman agrees to receive the drug on board his ship he pays about Rs. 130 per seer (three balls), but if he decides to risk taking it aboard himself he pays about Rs.. 100 per seer.

At the other end at Rangoon, Shanghai or Hong Kong, he receives anything from Rs. 160 to Rs. 200 per seer for the drug; consequently it can easily be seen what enormous profits can be made by an experienced smuggler. The rummagers and watchers of the Customs are always on the alert for smuggling; consequently the utmost caution has to be exercised in getting the stuff on board a vessel. The usual method of conveyance is a sampan or dinghy which is invariably used under cover of darkness and when tides are convenient, the occupants of which are ready to dump the balls overboard at a moment's notice should they be pursued.

Once the "dope" is on board, the novice usually finds his own hiding place, but once he is in the swim and becomes a member of a syndicate comprising smugglers of all ranks, European and Indian, things are easier. He would then pass the stuff on to, say, the engine room "serang" who would perhaps bury it deep down in the coal bunkers beneath tons and tons of coal in order to lessen the chances of detection.

That this plan is not always successful is shown by the fact that in September 1923 the Calcutta rummaging staff worked for five days more or less continually in the coal bunkers of the Indo-China steamer "Lai Sang," during which time they shifted something like three hundred tons of coal. They were successful in their efforts for they recovered no less than six hundred ounces of cocaine of a total value of Rs. 40,000, a serious blow to the smuggling fraternity. Another method of secretion is to float the opium on top of the water in the ballast tanks, a tin box fixed to a short plank being need for the purpose.

Shortly before a vessel leaves Calcutta for the Far East she is generally examined by a party of Customs' rummagers and this is when a novice at the smuggling game begins to get nervous, for every known corner and crevice is very carefully inspected, and, should the opium be hidden in a confined space, such as a cabin, for instance, it is quite possible that its peculiar odour would betray its presence to an experienced searcher. This search is repeated at Rangoon, Penang and Singapore, and should the "dope" escape detection, the smuggler, on the vessel arriving at Hong Kong or Shanghai, makes preparations to hand over the stuff according to a pre-arranged plan.

The usual procedure is to advise a "dope-agent" in the port to have a sampan ready on a certain night to glide down with the tide close to the ship's side. A dull thud is heard as the parcel is dropped from some obscure port-hole and the sampan glides quietly away.

It is not always disposed of in so easy a manner. Sometimes the smugglers endeavour to outwit the Customs men by placing one or two balls of opium in some corner of the after deck where they can be easily detected. When it is discovered the searchers usually gather to view the spot for future reference. This is the moment the smugglers have been waiting for and within a minute or two pounds and pounds of the drugs find their way over the ship's side on the forward well-deck and are quietly rowed away in sampans which have been waiting for that very purpose. Still another method adopted is for a khalasi (Indian seaman) to stumble up against one of the Customs men and try to provoke a quarrel. Blows are exchanged and the rest of the searchers run to the assistance of their comrade, so giving the smugglers the desired opportunity they have been waiting for.

So much for opium on the outward journey. After calling at Amoy and Moji the vessel will eventually arrive at Kobe, a town on the Inland Sea of Japan. Here the smuggler arranges on suitable terms for a supply of cocaine which eventually comes aboard the vessel in 25 oz. tins or in small bottles each containing from two to five ounces. The purchase price of cocaine in Kobe

A Dream of Hashish.

(By courtesy of "The Tatler")

varies, but is usually about seventeen yen per ounce (about Rs. 28). In Calcutta the selling price is from Rs. 45 to Rs. 60 per ounce. As a rule there are two qualities available, Japanese and German, the former being much the inferior of the two.

The Japanese Government is supposed to co-operate with other countries in the suppression of the cocaine traffic, but as it represents a lucrative source of revenue the precautions taken to prevent export are extremely lax, consequently the smuggler experiences little or no difficulty in getting his supply on board his ship.

The vessel is searched in every port of call just as it is with opium, and when it arrives in the Hooghly it is met by a Custom's boat which follows it right up to its moorings to prevent parcels being thrown overboard into dinghies. When the vessel anchors a search party boards her and watchers are stationed round the ship all the time she is in port.

It is not the usual practice to search officers when they are going ashore, but should a man be suspected he is liable to be stopped and searched at any time. As substantial rewards are offered for information that will lead to an arrest it is not uncommon for men to betray their confederates, though this of course applies chiefly to the native section of the crew.

As the reward offered to searches for locating contraband on a vessel is very small it is often the case that a hiding place will be left undisturbed in order to identify the owner. Should a smuggler happen to be caught with opium or cocaine his "dope-running" days are over, at any rate on this particular trade route.

I will now quote from an article by Major W. R. Foran in "Chambers Journal" in which the author, who has evidently an intimate acquaintance with the ways of smuggler and "dope" traffickers in India and Burma, describers the artfulness of these people and some of the awful effects these drugs have on their victims.

"As regards artfulness and ingenuity," the writer says, "the cleverest rogues in Europe could scarcely show greater resource than the "Dope traffickers" in India and Burma. To the generality of people the smuggler is a bold and bad man with fierce and heavily bearded face; and he is popularly credited with being armed to the teeth with knives pistols and other lethal accoutrements. In reality the smuggler—the Indian variety, at any rate, is nothing of the sort. To all outward appearance he is a respectable well-to-do and easy-going merchant: but he is a thorough-paced scoundrel for all that and his ostensible business activities are merely a blind to his real and secret occupation.

"A very good example of the truth of this statement came to my direct notice a year or two ago in Rangoon. I was seeking quaint curios to purchase as presents for friends in England and America and chanced to hear of a newly-opened Chinese shop in the Indian Bazaar quarter of the city; here, so I was informed, could be seen a marvellous selection of Chinese and Tibetan goods. These rare treasures were being sold at ridiculously low prices, and were fast disappearing; so I was urged to make a visit to this Chinese merchant with the least possible delay. The news seemed almost too good to be true, but I sallied forth to investigate.

"On arrival at the Chinaman's premises I was amazed at the remarkable range of the goods offered for sale; and still more so at the price marked on each article exposed to view. I had never seen such a wonderful collection of silks, linen, lace, embroidery, ivory articles and so forth, and it was with frank delight that I made the very most of this golden opportunity. As my eyes searched here and there in the gloom of the interior of the shop, I awoke to the fact that there was a steady stream of Chinese, Indian and Burmese customers passing through the building and that all seemed intent upon reaching the back premises. This set my thoughts wondering for it was unusual to find such a brisk trade in any shop of the Bazaar. Yet beyond this fact there was nothing to arouse suspicion except perhaps that the merchandise was priced absurdly low.

"I secured a splendid collection of gifts that would please all my friends enormously and then took my departure. It so happened that I was at a dinner-party that same evening and my host was a senior officer of the Imperial Police. In the course of conversation during dinner I told him of the wonderful luck that had chanced my way only that morning. It struck me as strange that he appeared to show little interest in my narrative; but I noticed a rather grim smile on his lips. When my tale was concluded he asked abruptly for the address of this wonderful shop. Quite innocently I gave him the information. Nothing more was said. I should have dismissed the matter then and there had it not been that on the following morning a fellow-guest at my hotel requested me to take him to this Chinaman's shop. On our arrival there we found it closed and some police on guard. It seems that John Chinaman was neither more nor less than an opium smuggler from Shanghai. He had brought all his shop's stock from China with him and had set up in legitimate business as a blind to his illegitimate activities; and, so I was told, had made a most profitable visit to Rangoon until the police discovered what he was doing. I consider myself very fortunate in having visited his place of business when I did."

Drug-taking in the Orient is almost second nature to the natives. I once asked a well-known doctor if opium-smoking was the dreadful thing it was generally thought to be. He answered me in both the affirmative and the negative. Excess in opium, he stated, is worse than in most things; but if he had to choose between opium and alcoholic excess he would unhesitatingly insist that drunkness was by far the worse evil. He summed up his opinion in the following words—

"Opium does not and never can degrade any man as drink does; and nobody makes a beast of himself with opium. It neither makes a nuisance of a man nor does it lead to violence and murder, as excess in alcohol does invariably."

As the result of many years' observation of people addicted to both vices I am inclined to believe that he is right.

Morphia is another vice in the Orient, although it is nothing like so prominent as the opium habit. Morphia injection in Eastern countries is far more repulsive than opium-smoking. I have visited dens where both vices were largely indulged and it is impossible to compare the former with any other drug vice; I would merely observe "May God have mercy upon votaries of morphia."

Cocaine is another drug with a big following in the Orient and it is an unmixed vice. Cocaine has a far greater power over its votaries than either morphia or opium for the after-distress is keener and the craving for more much stronger. A slave to cocaine is a slave indeed! The harm that it does and the certainty with which it eventually kills its victims are truly appalling. I have seen some really dreadful intances of confirmed cocaine-takers and there is nothing that can be done to cure them of this terrible vice.

Indulgence in hemp-smoking in India is as common as betel-chewing and tobacco-smoking. I have seen hemp being smoked everywhere that my wandering footsteps have taken me in India and also quite extensively in Burma and the Shan States. I have discussed this vice with many government officials and have discovered a wide diversity of opinion as to whether it is merely an undesirable form of indulgence without any permanently evil effects or whether it is gravely harmful. Personally I incline to the latter opinion, but I have no doubt at all that it can never be effectually stopped. Hemp-smoking is far too ingrained a habit amongst Indians to be ever successfully uprooted.

It seems apt to retail an old Persian allegory on the effects of these various Eastern vices that I came across during the course of my way-side wanderings in the Orient. It so correctly illustrates my view of the comparative degree of harm derived from the various drugs in common use East of Suez,' that it could not be bettered. This ancient allegory says: "Three men arrived one night at the closed gates of a Persian city. One man suffered from the effects of excessive alcohol drinking, the second from the effects of opium-eating and the third had smoked hemp to excess. Let us break down the gates of the city,' shouted the alcoholic drinker in a fury of drunken rage, for I can do it with my sword.' 'Nay,' sleepily protested the opium-eater, 'we can rest here outside the city in comfort. In the morning the gates will be opened and then we can enter. There is no hurry necessary.' 'Why all this foolish talk?' whined the hemp-smoker 'Let us all three creep through the key-hole.'"

GROWTH OF THE COCAINE HABIT.

A recent press report thus describes the growth of the cocaine habit in India and its introduction into Calcutta.

"A question asked with growing frequency by those interested in preventing the traffic in cocaine is whether it is impossible that the drug should be manufactured secretly in India. There is evidence that the cocaine habit is spreading rapidly in the country and yet no one has been able to trace the source from which the drug is obtained. Arrests of people in possession of packets are fairly frequent, but it is a strange fact that the majority have been arrested not coming off ships but stepping out of railway carriages. In Calcutta, foi instance, more cocaine smugglers have been discovered at Howrah than as passengers disembarking at the docks and jetties. There is the more reason to expect illicit manufacture in India because there is no difficulty in obtaining the coca leaf and the process of manufacture is not particularly expensive. Skill and the qualifications of a chemist are necessary to the manufacturer, but considering the large sums of money to be made and the facilities offered in Europe to those who desire technical equipment there is no real bar to the existence in India of one or more concerns for secretly producing cocaine.

The great point is that the leaf from which the extract is made does grow wild in the country. The older books state that the coca plant is only to be found in South America, but its cultivation has within recent years been extended to various parts of the older world. Sir George Watt in his "Commercial Products of India" prints a remarkable account of the introduction of the plant into this country and Ceylon. In 1870 the coca was brought to Ceylon from Kew. In 1876 at a committee meeting of the Agri-Horticultural Society of Madras a letter was read from Mr.

Joseph Steverton, who suggested the propagation of the plant "in view of the probability of this becoming an important article of commerce." No steps however were taken till 1885 when owing to discovery of the value of cocaine as an anaesthetic a demand for the leaf grew up in Europe. At this time the Agri-Horticultural Society of India distributed young plants from their Calcutta gardens to various tea-gardens. The Government of India also took an interest in the matter and Sir George Watt has unearthed a despatch addressed to the Secretary of State in which particulars about the method of preparing the leaf in use in South America are asked for.

Unlooked for consequences are said to have followed the introduction of the plant into India. The intention was no more than to have a Government plantation and factory under the strictest supervision, but the plants were distributed to various parts of India in order to discover where they would flourish best. It was found that coca would not bear frost and the plants sent to the cinchona plantations near Darjeeling proved a failure, but in Assam and Sylhet and on the slopes of the Nilgiris and in Madras the young seedlings flourished. Having seen it proved that the plant would grow in this country, the Government of India presently lost all interest in the experiment. Some planters seem to have adopted various means for drying and packing the leaves, possibly in the hope that there would be the same demand in India, as in Peru, for the article. The leaf has the peculiar effect of inhibiting the nerves of hunger in the stomach and it is for this reason that the Peruvian Indians chew it regularly. But this property was not known in India and so the planters found no sale for the leaf they maufactured. So they too lost interest in the matter. The plantations were left to themselves. Now the theory is that it is growing wild all over the country and that several classes of Indians have learnt something of the properties of the leaf and are chewing it as regularly as they do pan and betel.

There is a bad reaction from the effects of coca chewing. The Peruvian Indians are no better for the use they make of the leaf. Mastication is followed by a temporary accession of strength, but thereafter there is a great lassitude and further a craving that must be satisfied is created. In short the results of chewing the leaf only differ in degree from the results of taking cocaine as a drug. The suggestion then is two-fold. First, that there are secret factories of cocaine in India and, second, that whether there are factories or not Indians are learning the habit of chewing the leaf because the plant is growing wild all over the country. It might be difficult to substantiate the first assertion because secret factories naturally are secret, but if the coca plant is growing wild and the leaves are habitually masticated, surely there must be a sufficient number of educated persons to recognise the plant and point out the localities where it grows. Steps might then be taken to prevent the spread of a pernicious practice.

COCAINE DENS AND CLEVER DEVICES OF TRAFFICKERS.

This naturally leads to the question of cocaine dens and the clever devices used by traffickers in avoiding the police. That the traffic exists and is daily growing a greater menace to the health and prosperity of India, the following account amply proves. A recent statement made by Mr. E. H. Keays, Additional Chief Presidency Magistrate, Calcutta, to the effect that though cocaine was sold practically openly in certain parts of Calcutta the middleman and wholesale vendor were seldom brought to book has again called public attention to a serious social problem.

Cocaine was formerly introduced into India with little, if any restriction and it was only when the pernicious effects of the drug became apparent that the authorities took steps to regulate its distribution. Once a taste for cocaine has been acquired it does not easily lose its hold on its victim, whose craving for it has built up the extensive traffic in Calcutta and to a minor extent in the province.

The physiological effect of cocaine is not easy to analyse, although its baneful influences have only too often been proved. According to an officer who has made a close study of the subject the cocaine consumer feels that he is no longer part of what he regards as a very sordid world; but when the effects of the drug have worn off the vision is violently shattered and the state of the dreamer is a sad one. Physical degeneration is all rapid.

According to the last annual report of the Excise Department illicit traffic in cocaine is very prevalent in Calcutta. The habit shows undoubted signs of becoming popular in Dacca, particularly among some of the old Mohammedan families and reports of its use have come from Hooghly, Darjeeling and other places.

Japan and Germany are the chief sources of supply, Eastern crews being adept smugglers. They are not infrequently caught, but the odds are against the Customs and Excise staffs and large quantities of cocaine of the very best manufacture undoubtedly find their way into the market.

The problem with which Customs, Excise and Police authorities are at present grappling is one of wits rather than of force. In Calcutta cocaine traders have created a clever intelligence service which keeps them informed of any move which may lead to their detection, and their methods of concealment are elaborate. Cocaine dens kept by Kashmiris and Peshawaris are to be found in alleys and gullies in Northern Calcutta. Big, rambling houses, with perhaps forty or fifty rooms, are usually favoured as head-quarters. Spies are posted at all the entrances, and the approach of anyone likely to be connected with the Excise Department or Police is signalled by whistles or other means. Doors and windows are heavily bolted and barred, every obstacle being carefully prepared to prevent a sudden raid. On one occasion a policeman leading raid found that the staircase had been electrified and he not only got an unpleasant shock but gave the alarm.

It is said that those who buy cocaine at these dens often do not even see the person supplying the drug, which is passed through a trap-door, a secret panel or through a hole in the ceiling. The covered packet appears apparently from nowhere attached to a piece of cotton; the purchaser—the money part of the business has already been arranged—having little, if any knowledge of those actually running the business. The cocaine dealer, though a careful man, is not afraid to fight should occasion demand and it is on this account that houses have to be raided in force, thus eliminating the all-important element of surprise.

It is often possible to catch the hawker, but it is quite another matter to tackle a crafty Kashmiri, fortified by cunning strategy. When entrance is obtained to a den after exasperating delays the owner, plausible and polite, invites an inspection of his premises. Usually nothing incriminating to be found because he has had time to dispose of his stock. Cocaine, for instance, dissolves in water and it is kept in small packets which are easily concealed.

No evidence has been obtained despite exhaustive inquiries that the drug is manufactured in Bengal. Most of the seizures are made at the Ports. In 1928, out of about 1,400 ounces seized by the authorities, only 25 ounces were discovered outside, 23 ounces being found at Dacca.

Steps are being taken to get to grips with those really controlling the trade—their names in some cases are known. It is a mistake to suppose as might be gathered from the remarks of Mr.

Keays that efforts are not made to çapture the wholesale men. They are sometimes caught and brought to Court where some, after protracted trials, are acquitted and others escape with what are considered to be unduly light sentences. The police are, it is understood, not primarily responsible for the detection of cocaine smuggling. Their interest begin when the consumption of cocaine has a direct bearing on crime or when they are called upon to assist in a raid organised by the Excise Department.

This fact does emerge from an investigation of the circumstances that there is in Calcutta, at the moment a highly organized cocaine traffic, with strong financial resources and that the facilities at present available for dealing with it are inadequate."

CHINA TOWN
CALCUTTA
THE ENTRANCE OF THE TOONGOON CHURCH
A SCENE IN THE CHOW SHOP
A GLIMPSE INTO THE GAMBLING DEN
ONE OF THE FEW SHOPS WHICH KEEP OPEN IN THE DAY
THE CARDS USED AT THE DENS

CHAPTER IV.

THE LURE OF CHINA TOWN.

There is scarcely a city in India in which the Chinese element has not congregated in some particular quarter, creating there an atmosphere essentially Chinese in character. So marked is this change and so different in every essential from the ordinary city life that China Town soon becomes the rendezvous of rich and poor alike. Calcutta is no exception to this rule. We have in our local China Town Chinese Hotels de Luxe, but it is not to such places of amusement that I propose to introduce the reader. Chinese restaurants, *a la Anglaise,* are all very well in their way, but the impressions created are false and the "atmosphere" faked. I prefer the genuine article—miserable "Chop-houses," "Chow-shops" in which it is neither pleasant to remain nor safe to be too curious.

The easiest and shortest way into China Town is through Bow Bazar and Blackburn Lane. There are two small temples dedicated to Kali in Bow Bazar Street which serve as excellent landmarks. The first of these "Cheena Kali": so called from the fact that many Chinese here offer sacrifice to Kali, is the one that interests us at present. To the right of this temple is Blackburn Lane; follow this and your nose and five minutes will find you in the heart of China Town.

As I believe in first impressions let me describe my initial visit to this insalubrous quarter in company with a boon companion. Taking the usual route we soon arrived in the heart of the Chinese quarter. Here we left the main thoroughfare and turning down a bye-lane entered what was apparently a Restaurant and Saloon combined.

For the benefit of the uninitiated I will describe this Restaurant in detail. The interior consisted of a single room divided into three compartments, and lit by a vile-looking oil lamp which was suspended from the centre of the roof. The larger of these three rooms, was furnished with three oblong tables, ranged on both sides with wooden benches and ornamented with blue porcelain jars filled with chop-sticks. The walls were decorated with newspaper illustrations and photographs of actresses in various stages of *deshabille,* while little moral maxims in gilded characters on a red ground informed the public of the praise worthy characteristics of the proprietor and the numberless blessings in store for the lucky people who patronised him. This room served the dual purpose of a *salle-a-manager* and kitchen. Of the other two rooms, one was the proprietor's sanctum and the other was a small enclosure, fitted with a table which served for a Bar, the counter and an altar for his various *penates dei* before whom a few joss-sticks burned incessantly.

On entering we were courteously greeted by the proprietor, who made room for us at the table by the very simple expedient of bundling a few of his erst-while guests into the street. I strove my hardest to ingratiate myself with him and so far succeeded that after a while he became quite communicative. I learned his history (probably invented for my special benefit). He had been a sailor and had travelled all over the civilised globe, but had settled down in Calcutta, where he informed me Chinamen were better treated than in any other part of the world. He spoke excellent English and from him I learned some queer customs of these peculiar people. The practice in vogue in Calcutta of calling every Chinaman "John" irrespective of his class and station in life is particularly offensive. Chinese etiquette requires that in addressing a stranger each should compliment the other and everything belonging to him in the most laudatory style at the same time depreciating himself and all his belongings to the lowest possible point. The following is no exaggeration, though not the precise words:

"What is your Honour's distinguished appellation?"

"My insignificant name is Wong."

"Where is your magnificent palace situated?"

"My contemptible hut is in Calcutta."

"How many are your illustrious beautiful children "

"My vile, worthless, idotic brats are five."

"How is the health of your distinguished spouse?"

"My mean, good-for-nothing old hag of a wife is well."

It was here I was also destined to get my first real insight into the true Chinese character. While conversing with the proprietor, I noted that he rose and bowed courteously to a venerable looking Chinaman who had just entered his shop, and whose station in life appeared to be far above the usual class who frequented this eating-house. I enquired who the stranger was and learning that he was a distinguished Doctor-at-Law, very much respected in this quarter for his erudition, I soon found an opportunity for addressing him. The learned Doctor replied courteously enough to all my enquiries respecting his health, but, I felt that in order to draw him out I must get him inveigled into a controversy on some knotty problem of the Law. In vain I racked my brain for something sufficiently oriental to interest him. At last an old tale, over which I had often puzzled in my College days occurred to me and I determined to try its effect on him. "Honoured Sir," I began, "will you decide for me this complicated question? A Chinaman died, leaving his property by will to his three sons, as follows: "To Fun Hum the eldest, one-half thereof; to Nu-Pin, his second son, one third thereof; and to Ding-Bat, his youngest, one-ninth thereof."

When the property was inventoried it was found to consist of nothing more nor less than seventeen elephants and it puzzled these three heirs how to divide the property according to the terms of the will without chopping up the seventeen elephants and thereby seriously impairing their value. Finally they applied to a wise neighbour, Sum-Punk, for advice. Sum-Punk had an elephant of his own. He drove it into the yard with the seventeen and said. "Now we will suppose that your father left these eighteen elephants. Fun-Hum take your half and depart."

So Fun-Hum took nine elephants and went his way.

"Now, Nu-Pin" said the wise man "take your third and git."

So Nu-Pin took six elephants and travelled.

"Now Ding-Bat" said the wise man, "take your ninth and begone."

So Ding-Bat took two elephants and absquatulated.

Then Sun Punk took his own elephant and drove home again. "Now" concluded I with a fine flourish, striving to emphasize my point and so stir his professional zeal, "was the property divided according to the terms of the Will?" For fully a minute the old gentleman did not stir. Then without a word he turned and gazed at me curiously as if I were some interesting anthropological specimen and as silently left the shop. Fortunately I know when I am beaten, I paid the bill and did likewise.

My companion now decided to take a hand in the game. Through various alleys he piloted me till we found ourselves in company with several vile looking specimens of humanity in a long, low, dingy room filled with men and smoke, but no noise. At first from the general hush I was under the impression that we had entered the anti-chamber of some Chinese Temple, but I soon discovered that we were in one of those interesting places known as Gambling Dens. I will not attempt to describe my surroundings as the table and its contents immediately engrossed my attention. In order that the Chinese idea of gambling may be understood, it is necessary to have some knowledge of the game.

There are several systems of gambling. There is the well-known Fan-Tan, a game much resembling the older system of Dice, but the game in progress as we entered had so many points of interest about it and was so redundant with surprise for the novice that its description will prove quite illuminating. There are twelve cards, little slips of Bamboo paper on which are printed weird and incomprehensible characters. The cards represent the following: A black and red Queen, a black and red King, a black and red carriage, a black and red elephant, a black and red dragon and lastly, a black and red gun. The victim arms himself with a pack of these cards, takes his stand besides the table and the fleecing process begins. Before proceeding further let me state definitely that I have nothing to say against the Chinese systems of gambling, they are as fair and above-board as any European system and better than most. If you lose its your luck, nothing more.

An old Chinaman stands at the head of the table and drones out this soul-stirring narrative. "Once there was a Queen."—Down goes a card. (You think hard. "Yes, I've got it. Its the Red queen" and you lay your own card down) and she went out riding,"—another card. (Immediately your brain is working, nineteen to the dozen. Yes, you have it. She goes out riding in the black carriage, or can it be the red carriage? Impossible it must be the red elephant or the black?), "and on the way she meets,"—down goes another card. "Heaven! I haven't decided that last point yet. She meets the King of course, but which King, the red or the black? Or perhaps she met the dragon, or perhaps the other Queen? Confound it, she may have met the other elephant or even the other carriage) "and together they go to see" another card. (Lord, there goes another card. Now what could they have gone to see. It's possible she met the black queen and saw the dragon. No, that would be too much for the old girl's nerves. She must have met the black King and seen the dragon. Of course it is possible she may have met the dragon and seen the king, but which King and which dragon? Or could it be the elephant she met and saw the King on it? Or it may be "and together they fled to"—another card. (Heavens, there goes the fourth card. Why I'm getting positively nervous." You make a desperate effort to steady yourself and to collect your scattered wits. You begin again. The red queen or perhaps the black one goes out riding on the red or black elephant or in the red or black carriage and on the way she meets the red or black King or perhaps the red or black dragon or perhaps the red or black carriage or perhaps the red or black elephant or perhaps) "and on the way they meet," another card. (Lord? Again they meet something. Now let me think. Why of course. It's a runaway match. The red queen goes in a black carriage and meets the black King, they elope together but on the way they meet the Black Queen—Hurrah! I've got it this time, the Heathen Chinese can't do me.") "and they shoot it with," —another card. For a moment you feel stunned. No process of reasoning can elucidate this impossible problem. Your head is aching, your nerves gone. You look around miserably excepting to see the same despair on every face but you are met with that calm stoicism so characteristic of the Chinese. Utterly crushed you move stealthily away from the table with an apologetic smile or pretend you have urgent business elsewhere and so escape.

There are of course other tables and other games, one in particular interested me. It consisted in a game much resembling Roulette only that the place of the revolving disk was taken by dice. You put your money down on any particular figure that strikes your fancy, the Banker throws, and if you are fortunate enough to have the winning number you get 10 to 1 on your money. This delightful simplicity appealed to me. The whole system was so obviously fair: I followed the game closely and observed that one man won continuously. By some uncanny intuition he seemed to divine the winning number each time. His performance filled me with admiration. I drew my companion's attention to his wonderful and continuous luck. To all intents and purposes the rest of the players appeared to be putting down their money just for the pleasure of seeing him rake in the shekels. I was however considerably mortified to learn that this paragon was the owner of the table. However just at that moment I had a brain wave. Why not follow his luck and so share some of the spoils. I looked around suspiciously to see if my companion had divined my intentions. He was smoking gazing absent-mindedly at the roof. Reassured I determined to carry my intentions into effect. I recollected I still had that five "dib" note left and heroically determined to risk the lot. The play was resumed. I watched the owner put his money on a "3." The psychological moment had arrived. Down went my hand into my trouser pocket for that note. "Hullo. Why, of course, I must have put it in the other pocket. No, there's nothing there." I began to grow uneasy. Hurriedly I searched my coat pockets, my vest-coat pockets and then back again to my trouser pockets. "No, that elusive note was not to be found." Once again I made my rounds, visiting every post in turn, but alas! the note was gone. Realizing the awful truth, I confided my suspicions in an awe-inspiring whisper to my companion. With an enigmatic smile this satellite of mine took my arm and led me, a crestfallen creature, from this den of iniquity, but on the threshold I heard him quote, *sotto voice*:—

"Which is why I remark
And my language is plain
That for ways that are dark
And for tricks that are vain
The heathen Chinese is peculiar;
Which the same I am free to maintain."

From here curiosity drove us to see that *piece de resistance* of all Chinese curiosities, an Opium

Den. The result was disappointing. I had read De Quincey's "Opium-Eater" and nerved myself in anticipation of some revolting scenes of debauchery. But alas the Chinaman in Calcutta takes his opium like a gentleman. It is true it gives him his quietus in the usual orthodox fashion, but there is nothing bizzare and unique in seeing a couple of old emaciated Chinaman asleep. The appearance of an opium den is curious enough, but it would be far more interesting if there were a little more light on the subject. The trade is undeniably suffering from a slump as the old bedlamite at the entrance informed us. The cruel Government had put up the price of opium so high that the poor Chinaman could not even have his smoke and in her opinion—"A Chinaman's as fine a man as any other kind of man."

We looked into a couple of these places. They are all got up more or less on the same principle devoid of all furniture, with the exception of a few rugs or mats scattered on the floor for the convenience of visitors who are "spending the night." In one corner, seated on a low stool, with a tray full of pipes before him, a small uncovered lamp and a little china pot in which he keeps the opium, sits the proprietor. As you enter he heats some of the opium, fills one of the pipes, lights a long taper and then hands them both to you. The opium is inhaled by holding the lighted end of the taper to the bowl of the pipe containing the opium and taking a succession of long steady whiffs. The pipes are of two descriptions. One, a bamboo or wooden pipe with a small bowl and a long stem, the other is constructed on the same principle but is made of metal and has an additional bowl containing water much after the fashion of the Indian Hookha.

I should like to pause here in my description of Opium Dens (of which I have much to say later) and indulge in a little folk-lore. As I said before to understand the Indian one must know something of his moral and spiritual outlook. No Indian—I refer to the ignorant masses mainly—considers the smoking of opium, ganja or bhang a vicious habit. If his holy men—yogis, rishis and fakirs smoke it, why should not he? I can imagine the consternation in any English parish in which the Pastor indulged in a little public opium smoking and yet in India, in the shade of the sacred "pepul" tree, on the steps of some old-world temple, sits a Yogi and smokes his "Ganja" and the reverent masses pass him by, wondering greatly what glorious visions have been vouchsafed to their holy man. It is perhaps incomprehensible to the Western mind and it is for this reason that I have digressed to relate a little folklore—mythical and truly Indian in its conception, but nevertheless acceepted as authentic by the illiterate villager—its perusal may help the reader to readjust his outlook.

CHAPTER V.

THE ORIGIN OF OPIUM.

Once upon a time there lived on the banks of the Ganges a holy Sage or Rishi who devoted his life to the performance of religious rites and to meditation. From dawn to dark he sat on the banks of the sacred stream engaged in devotion, crawling back to the palm-leaf hut he had built for himself when he needed a few hour's sleep. The spot he chose was miles away from human habitation and he was the only human being for miles around. His sole companion in his loneliness was a field-mouse that had taken up its quarters in his hut and lived on the leavings of his supper. The mouse seemed to know that its life was secure as the Sage was forbidden to take life and in consequence it stayed; as days passed it went up to the Sage, touched his feet and played with him. The Rishi alive to these friendly overtures and feeling the want of someone to talk to determined to give his little friend the power of speech. One night the mouse sitting on his hind-legs and holding his fore-legs up in a supplicating manner reverently said to the Sage "Master, you have very kindly given me the power of speech, but you have left me defenceless against the cat who visits your hut when you are employed at your devotions and who would have eaten me long ago, had it not been for the fear of angering you. I go about in fear all day lest this should happen and at the risk of annoying you I ask you, Master, to turn me into a cat so that I may fight and overcome my enemy." The Rishi filled with pity for the little rodent sprinkled Holy Ganges water over him and immediately the mouse was changed into a cat. A few nights after the Rishi asked the cat how he liked the change. "Not much" replied the cat. "Are you not strong enough to hold your own against all the cats in the world?" asked the Sage. "True, Your Reverence, I can overcome any cat in the world but have new enemies who molest me when you are away and by their loud barking they frighten the life out of me. If it will not displease you make me into a dog, Master." "Be a dog then," replied the Rishi and immediately the change was effected.

A few nights after when darkness had set in the Rishi returned to the hut and sitting down said to the dog "Well, how is it now?" "Master, I cannot thank you enough for all your kindness. I was a mouse and you gave me speech and at my request turned me into a cat and then into a dog; as a dog I suffer no end of trouble for want of sufficient food; my only food is the leavings of your supper which is insufficient to satisfy my enlarged appetite. I am filled with envy at the apes when I see them jumping from tree to tree and eating the delicious fruits that grow on them; pray do not be angry at my request to be turned into an ape."

The kind Rishi granted the request and the dog became an ape. The ape was wild with joy, leaping from tree to tree eating the luscious fruit growing on them. His joy however was short-lived, for with the approach of summer there came a drought. As a monkey our friend found it hard to drink from the rivers and pools as these were infested by wild boars splashing in the cool waters all day . That night he recounted to the Sage the difficulties of his state as an ape and the pleasures he had seen surrounding the lives of wild boars and earnestly begged to be transformed into a boar. The Sage whose knidness was boundless complied with the request and turned the ape into a boar. For two whole days the boar revelled in splashing in the streams and pools but on the next he received a rude shock, for the Raja of the country was out hunting wild boars and several had fallen to his unerring aim and our friend just escaped by the skin of his teeth, a bullet having just missed him giving him food for reflection on the dangers surrounding a boar's life. In the suite of the Raja there was one thing that had struck his eye and it was the gaily caparisioned elephants that the Raja and his suite rode. He longed to be an elephant and at night through the kindness of the Rishi of whom he requested the change he became an elephant. He was roaming in the forest when one day he again saw the Raja with a large following enter the jungle in search of sport and the Raja saw him and admired him on account of his beauty and greatly desired to possess him. The next day an elephant hunt was organised and our friend caught. The matter of taming and training was easy and the elephant soon became the favourite in the stud and carried the Rajá on many occasions. One day the Rani expressed a desire to bathe in the sacred waters of the Ganges and the Raja hearing of her intentions expressed his intention of accompanying her. Orders were issued for the newly-caught elephant to be saddled and brought. The animal approached and simultaneously with his Mahout saluted the royal couple. The Raja and Rani mounted and anyone would imagine our friend would have been proud to have been chosen from among so many *hatis* for this duty. But no. There was a fly in the ointment. The animal filled with pride at being at last changed into a lordly beast could not tolerate the idea of a woman riding on his back, although she was a queen. This was degradation indeed and in his hurt pride he stood up with such suddenness that the royal couple were thrown to the ground. The king jumped up, picked up the queen and tried to console her, asking her if she was hurt and offering to do anything for her. The elephant after doing the mischief stood apart watching the concern of the king. Filled with envy he turned round and bolted to the forest and there under the shade of a banyan tree reflected thus:—After all, I see that a queen is the happiest of all creatures and of great and infinite regard; he thereupon determined to ask to be changed. At sunset he arrived at the hut on the river bank and stood before it with hanging head. "What's the news and why have you left the king's stud?" asked the Rishi. The elephant answered "All I asked of thee, Master, you have graciously granted me and I have one and only one more boon to crave of you. As an elephant my bulk has increased but not my happiness. To-day I have seen that of all creatures a queen is the happiest. Oh, holy Reverence, make me a queen." Puzzled at the request the Sage asked "How can I make you into a queen; how and where am I to get a kingdom for you and a royal husband into the bargain? All I can do for you is to change you into the most beautiful girl that stepped on the earth and put my trust in the gods to grant you an interview with some great Prince." The elephant agreed and the change was immediately effected and the Sage gave her the name of Postomani or poppy-seed lady.

Postomani lived in the Rishi's hut and spent her time tending the flowers and watering the plants. One day after she had finished her occupation she was seated at the door when a stranger richly clad came up to her. She stood up and faced him enquiring who he was and what he wanted. The stranger whom Postomani rightly suspected was the king of the country answered he had been out hunting and had been chasing a deer and was thirsty. Seeing the hut of the hermit he had come for some refreshments. Postomani excused herself for the poor fare she had to offer and entering the hut returned with a ghurra (waterpot) and approaching the stranger she made as if she would wash his feet. "Not so, fair maid" said the king stepping back "I am a Kshatriya and thou the daughter of a holy Sage: it is not meet for thee to wash my feet." "I am not the Rishi's daughter nor am I a Brahman girl, so there can be no harm in my touching your feet. Remember you are my guest and I am bound by the laws of hospitality to wash your feet." "What is your caste then" asked the stranger. "The Rishi tells me my parents, now dead, were Kshatriyas."

The king came often and made love to the girl and one day they were married by the Rishi. She became the favourite wife of the Raja. Standing against the parapet of a well talking to her husband one morning she suddenly became giddy and before the Raja could put out a hand to help her she fell into the well and died. The Raja was inconsolable, the Rishi tried all in his power to make him forget. "Grieve not" he said "for the past, that which is fixed by fate must come to pass. The queen just drowned is not of royal blood, she was born a rat and went through several changes before becoming the elephant that threw the queen and you off its back. Now that she is gone take into favour your former queen. As for my reputed daughter through the favour of the gods I will make her name immortal. Let her body rest in the well, fill the well with earth and try and forget her. Out of her flesh and bones will a tree grow in the well which shall be called Posto, i.e. the poppy-tree: from this tree will the drug called opium be obtained which will be celebrated as a powerful medicine throughout the ages and which will be either swallowed or smoked as a powerful narcotic to the end of time. The opium addict will have one quality of each of the animals to which Postomani was transformed . He will be mischievous as a rat, fond of milk as a cat, quarrelsome as a dog, filthy as an ape, savage as a boar, slow as an elephant and high-tempered as a queen. Grieve not, O king."

(Top) Dhakin Rai, God of the Harvest.
(Below) Tapping the Date Palm.

CHAPTER VI.

WORSHIP OF RURAL DEITIES.

Calcutta like most big cities is visited frequently by villagers who come to see "the sights". in this City of Palaces and the amazement, the incredulous, gaping wonder of their expression, as they slowly and timidly wander down the principal thoroughfares is an amusing, if familiar sight to most Ditchers. But these people are not the simple, unsophisticated folk we fondly believe them to be. They are capable of driving as shrewd a bargain as the thriftiest city dweller and the uncanny skill and dexterity with which they evade the tax-collector and Excise Laws place them on a par with the Marwari, that King of Financiers of whom it is said, and I believe truthfully, that he leaves his home a beggar, provided only with a "lota" (brass water-pot) and a string wherewith to draw water from his neighbour's well and returns, a few years later, a prince among his people. How does he do it? Ask Clive Street and The Exchange. But to return to the "dehati" or villager.

"MOONSHINERS" IN BENGAL.

Rural Bengal is the home of the original "moonshiner". In no other part of India is this lucrative profession carried on with more impunity and with greater advantage. There is not a village, hamlet or hut in the interior and less frequented parts of this district that has not its own private brewery or it's local suri-khana (literally grogshop) to which the sturdy labourer after his day's toil in the field comes for his evening "drop."

The villager in Bengal has found from bitter experience that the commodity sold as "tea" in his native village is a very much overrated beverage and one that is entirely unsuited to his constitution and methods of life.

Of the non-intoxicating liquors drunk in rural Bengal the best known are "dab", the water contained in the green cocoanut and toddy, the fresh juice of the date palm. Of intoxicants we have several, the commonest being "taru" or "daru," "arrack" and several cheap brands of locally distilled imitations of foreign brews.

Toddy, being a natural product and cheap, is greatly in demand and a considerable revenue is earned by landowners who hire out the date palms growing on their lands for toddy tapping. The modus operandi is simple. The juice of the date palm flows easily and is collected at night. An incision is first made with a *dao* in the trunk of the tree a little below the leaves. A split palm leaf is next inserted into the cut and helps to drain off the juice into an earthen pot tied to the tree immediately below the incision. All night the juice flows into this jar which by morning is practically full. It is strained and drunk in its natural condition. In this state it is known as "Khajur-Russ" and is a harmless, bitter-sweet beverage possessing many medicinal virtues. Later in the day, however, as the heat increases the juice ferments and soon becomes a mildly inotxicating liquor known as "taru" or "daru". In its fermented condition the taste is very similar to light Pilsener beer and in this form it is consumed in vast quantities by the local villagers, particularly on Sundays and festivals. The Bengal rustic is a convivial fellow and large earthen-ware pots (Chatties) containing three to four gallons of taru are frequently purchased by parties of four to five who convey it to some secluded spot where they sit round it for hours, drinking, singing and dancing far into the night.

"Arrack" is a more potent spirit of local manufacture. It is distilled from fermented rice-water to which are added several ingredients to hasten the fermentation. It possesses highly intoxicating qualities and to it may be traced many of the sensational crimes committed in these districts. Its consumption seems to be confined to the lower caste, such as the domes, mughs, etc.

It is interesting to note how the source and the use of some of these intoxicants find a place among the *penates dei* and the ritual of the Hindu. The date palm from which he received his favourite beverage is sacred to the goddess "Chandi"—a form of Durga, Shiva's consort, who is supposed to reside within this palm.

The worship of this goddess takes a somewhat unusual and seemingly irreverent form. It will frequently be noticed that in a grove of date palms, while the majority of trees bear traces of having been tapped, there are usually one or two that are left untouched.

There are the trees dedicated to the worship of the goddess Chandi. The ceremonial is very simple. When a cultivator wishes to propitiate the goddess he proceeds to a spot where one of these date trees stand. Here he places himself about fifty feet or so away from the palm. He then calls aloud to the goddess bidding her heed and answer his prayers. With this the initial part of his worship is completed. He then proceeds with the more practical part of finding out whether the goddess is prepared to answer his prayers. To ascertain this he collects a number of clods of earth. Armed with these missiles he calls out a wish and then throws a clod at the palm. If his marksmanship is equal to the occasion and he records a hit it is a sign that the goddess is prepared to grant him that particular wish: if not, he concludes that the contrary is the case and then proceeds with the second wish and so on till he exhausts his supply of missiles or concludes that he has asked enough favours for that day. This strange practice accounts for the mottled appearance of these trees, which are practically covered with clods of earth.

In certain parts of Bengal where this system of tree worship is very much in vogue and where the rustic is of a superior class, the throwing of mud clods is done away with and offerings of sweets, fruits and herbs are made to propitiate the goddess, the worship of whom is supposed to obtain for the devotee immunity from disease, success in litigation, etc.

There is another god whose worship is very dear to the heart of the cultivator. This is Dhakin-rai, the god of the fields. His appearance is extremely singular and is intended to convey the idea of growth. This peculiar formation will be found to correspond very closely with that of the ears of wheat and the budding Indian corn.

The principal duties of this deity are to provide rain, to produce a good and seasonable crop and to keep away pig and other wild animals that devastate these crops. In this last he is eminently succcessful as his anything but amiable features prove a very effective "scare-crow". The principal puja of Dhakin-rai falls on the 15th of January each year and it is significant that rain usually falls on or about that time . Occasionally when rain does not fall during this period the god is brought out of the village and left in an exposed place in the blazing heat of the sun, as a kind of gentle hint. Grain, fruits, flowers and occasionally fowls are offered during this puja. On special occasions when the harvest has been plentiful and there is much rejoicing in the villages Dhakin-rai is persuaded to take a part in the revels and is doused from head to foot in copious draughts of toddy.

Dhakin-rai, like most village deities, suffers the fate of all such gods whose worship only pertains to certain periods of the year. Once the harvest is over he is promptly forgotten and his effigy left in the parched and arid fields where it slowly crumbles to dust or alas! provides an excellent target for the juvenile part of the population.

"PIR" OR SAINT WORSHIP.

I cannot leave this interesting subject of the worship of deities, indigenous to our rural population, without commenting on another form of worship which pertains principally to the Moslem section of our rustic neighbours. This is the worship of "Pir" or Saints.

Recently in the very heart of Calcutta we had an illustration of how hard these customs die among the illiterate masses.

Calcutta during October 1924 was agog with excitement over the discovery of a new saint and now that he is dead and no longer capable of demonstrating them, numerous tales are being circulated regarding the wonderful powers this man possessed. Data Sahib, the Saint in question, has been declared a Pir by the Mahomedan butchers of the New Market Meat Stalls and has been buried in one of the main thoroughfares of the Market on the very spot selected by him during his lifetime of begging. It now appears that this Data Sahib was a Native Christian, a Madrassi by birth and a murderer, that he served a period of about 14 years in the Andamans, was released and subsequently reconvicted for theft, escaped and when too old for further villiany, took to begging as a lucrative profession.

The incidents that led up to this sudden canonization are remarkable. When it was reported to the market authorities that Data Fakir was dead orders were immediately issued for the removal of his body to the local Mahomedan burial ground. To this the Mahomedan butchers in the New Market objected on the grounds that according to an ancient custom a fakir was invariably buried on the spot on which he died. Very naturally the market authorities refused to sanction this and the butchers hit upon an ingenious method for coercing them. Four stalwart butchers proceeded to the spot and attempted to raise the bier on which the corpse was laid. After struggling for some time they informed the astonished on-lookers that it was immovable. Excitement ran high. Crowds began to collect. Ten, twenty, thirty men (all butchers) next assayed to lift the bier. Impossible. Moulvis and mullas from adjoining mosques came rapidly to the spot and hearing of this miraculous occurrence began enthusiastically to extol the saintly qualities of the deceased. By this time thousands had collected to view the body of the saint and then some brainy youth conceived the idea of a collection. It speaks volumes for the ignorance, credulity and generosity of Indian masses that within about two hours over Rs. 50,000 had been collected. The butchers now realising that old Data Sahib had become a valuable commercial asset determined on a bold move. In a body they approached the Corporation and demanded that the saint should be buried on the spot on which he sat during his life-time and although such a proceeding was wrong in principle, deplorable as a precedent and a grave public danger, permission was granted. This is another glaring instance of the success of mob law in this country, the inevitable after-math of the policy of non-co-operation.

This puts me in mind of the worship of Pir Gazi Sahib, a tutelary saint of the Sunderbans, the legends in connection with whom make interesting reading. It appears that the district around Bauripur was once a dense jungle infested with tigers and other wild beasts and here in a secluded spot dwelt Mobrak Gazi, a local fakir, whose penchant was his ability to overlord the beasts of the jungle and this he did so successfully that he went about riding a huge tigress. It once happened that the Zemindar of the district being unable to pay the revenue was arrested and cast into prison by order of the Emperor. The mother of the zemindar appealed to Mobrak Gazi for help. The Pir that night appeared to the Emperor in a dream and demanded the release of the zemindar threatening him with dire consequences if he refused, but offering to pay the revenue himself if the zemindar was set at liberty. The Emperor awoke and had the dream written down, but paid no heed to the warning. The next morning when he ascended his throne, instead of the usual courtiers, he found himself surrounded with ferocious beasts. In great alarm he immediately ordered the release of the zemindar who hastened home and informed his mother of all that had happened and together they went to see the Pir. Mobarak Gazi refused all rewards pointing instead to a spot where his treasures were buried, he bade them pay the revenue and accept the rest. He then vanished. In gratitude for his deliverance the zemindar proceeded to erect a mosque to the honour of Mobarak Gazi, but the saint appeared to him saying that he preferred living in the jungles and helping those who asked his protection. He thus became the patron saint of the wood-cutters, fishermen and

A Snake Worshipper at Prayer.

A Shrine in the heart of the forest.

others who frequent wild uninhabited parts of the Sunderbands.

Mobarak Gazi or as he is better known as Gazi Sahib is now worshipped throughout the Sunderbands and the form this worship takes is very peculiar. Before going into the forests the wood-cutters summon the local fakir and this worthy precedes the wood-cutters to the place they have selected to work in. Here he clears a small portion of the brush-wood and erects seven small huts with sticks and leaves. Beginning on the right the first hut is dedicated to Jagabandhu, the friend of the world: the second to Mahadeva, the destroyer; the third to Mansa, the snake goddess. Next to it a small platform is erected in honour of Rupapari, a jungle sprite who leads wayfarers astray. The next hut is divided into two compartments, one for Kali and the other for her daughter Kalimaya. The remaining huts are dedicated consecutively to Opari, goddess of the birds; Mamaswari and Burhi Thakurani together in the next and the last two containing two compartments each to Gazi Sahib and his brother Kaku and the last to his son Shawal Pir and his nephew Ram Gazi. The offerings made to these deities consist of fruits, vegetables, rice, etc., chiraghs are lit before the huts, pots of water covered with mango leaves and decorated with the image of the deity in vermillion are placed on the ground and flags hung over the huts.

When everything is ready the fakir retires to bathe and smears his body with vermillion. He then returns and folding his hands before his face goes down on his knees for a few minutes before the hut of each deity whose protection he supplicates in turn. This done the fakir rises and in order to ascertain whether there are any tigers in the vicinity he spans his arm from the elbow to one of the fingers. If the span fails to fit the finger exactly it means that there is a tiger in the vicinity and special spells have to be said to drive it off. These spells consist in an incantation on the following lines: "Dust, dust, the finest dust be in thine eyes, Oh! tiger and tigress. May thy eyes be blinded and thine ears stopped by the power of Gazi Sahib, etc." Similar incantations are said to bind the jaws of crocodiles.

So sure are the wood-cutters and fishermen of the potency of these spells that the name of Gazi Sahib said aloud is considered sufficient to scare away a tiger. Needless to say the mortality caused by tigers among these poor people is appalling.

CHAPTER VII.

THE WORSHIP OF SERPENTS.

I have mentioned Manasa, the snake goddess, as one of the tutelary deities of the Sunderbands, but her sphere of activity extends even to the common ryot who implores her protection when he goes to work in the fields. Like most gods there is a legend in connection with Manaṣa which I give as it explains the peculiar attitude of the villager to his most deadly foe.

It had happened that King Parikshit, the father of Janmejaya (and grandson of Yudhisthira), while hunting one day lost sight of a stag which he had pierced with an arrow and in his wanderings to trace it was overcome with fatigue and thirst when he met a Rishi who was in deep meditation. He requested the Rishi to provide him with food and water, but the Rishi made no reply and the King placed round the neck of the silent one a dead snake which was lying by.

The King went back to his capital without suspecting the full result of what he had done. The son of the Rishi construing the act as an insult to his father cursed the King and he met his death within a week by being bitten by a snake.

King Parikshit was succeeded by his son Janmejaya who determined to exterminate the whole snake-world and with this object, aided by Brahmans, planned a sacrifice. The result was the dire destruction of snakes which, with one exception, were all consumed in the sacrificial fire. The exception was Vasuki, the King of Serpents, whose life was spared.

As a reward the King of Serpents promised that henceforth anybody who would remember the name of Astika would have no trouble from snakes. Manasa or Jaratkaru, the mother of Astika—the saviour of serpents—received her due share of worship and since that day she is worshipped annually by her numerous devotees.

MYSTERIOUS RITES AND PRACTICES OF SNAKE DOCTORS.

Snake worshippers, however, have not confined themselves to propitiatory offerings. Finding that divine intervention was not always successful in genuine cases of snake-bite they set about studying various remedies that would save them from this awful scourge—the method, par excellence, was of course wizardry.

The rites in this connection take various forms. We are all familiar with the reputed properties of certain magic roots and stones, but the method described in the case below, reported in the "Statesman" of the 19th May, 1928, is so typical that I give the account in full.

"For two days "magicians" have performed over a body in Calcutta in a vain effort to restore life.

The scene of this tragi-comedy, based on

fervent belief in the supernatural powers of ojas (Indian sorcerers) is a mud hut in South Road, Entally, where there lived a barber called Chandwa Hajam.

About midnight on Monday the other persons sleeping in the bustis were roused by shrieks from the hajam who complained that he had been bitten by a snake. The hajam's toe was bleeding but upon a search being made for the snake no trace of it could be seen.

Following the custom among lower class Indians a mystery man known as an *oja* was summoned. The *oja* solemnly incanted his black magic and performed mysterious rites, but the hajam died before dawn.

The news travelled through the neighbourhood, more *ojas* were sent for and efforts to bring him back to life were redoubled. *Ojas* from far and near arrived at the hut next day. They refused to accept defeat, persisting that if only the snake that had bitten the hajam could be brought back and made to suck the poison away from the body, life would return.

The head-man among the *ojas* accordingly took five cowries and cast them in the four directions of the compass. The fifth he threw skywards. It was worked out that wherever the snake then was one of the cowries must strike it on the head and bring it back to the man's death-bed. The *oja* would then compel the snake to suck the poison out of its victim's body.

The mystery men waited patiently but nothing happened. Neither the snake nor the cowries returned, and the body of the snake-bitten man remained lifeless. A consultation took place among the *ojas,* who still refused to admit defeat, and eventually they declared that the snake must have been sent to poison the hajam by one bearing a grudge against him who had performed *jadu* (witch-craft) on the snake. They decided therefore, that unless the dead man's enemy was brought into the presence of his victim's body, there was no hope of his being restored to life.

His neighbours thereupon recalled that the dead man had had a business rival in the district, one Raghubir, also a barber, and suggested that he it must have been who sent the snake to him.

A call was made on Raghubir, who was brought to the deceased's bustee, where he was confronted with the body of his alleged victim.

The unfortunate Raghubir was openly charged by the men with having sent the snake to his rival. He stoutly denied, and expressed deep sorrow that his business rival was dead. The *ojas* refused to take his word and told Raghubir that he would have to bring his victim back to life. Again Raghubir's protestation of innocence was in vain, and he was compelled by the *ojas* to practise elaborate adjurations over the body with the object of exorcising the snake poison. This happened on Tuesday night.

Another attempt to restore the dead man was made next day but the neighbours then said it was useless to attempt to bring the barber back to life and informed the police. The body had then remained in the hut for nearly two days.

At noon on Wednesday the body was removed by the police to the morgue for post-mortem examination but owing to decomposition no definite opinion regarding the cause of death could be given.

Raghubir was brought to the local thana by the enraged *ojas* and neighbours, but after again protesting his innocence he was allowed to go home."

From the foregoing it will naturally be concluded that all such reputed cures from snake-bite are a hoax. I am not prepared to endorse such an opinion. India is a land of mystery and for those who seek there is much that will justify a very guarded opinion on mysterious cures of this description. I have witnessed "Snake Doctors" at work on a moribund case of snake-bite and have been compelled to admit a cure; but as third party evidence is more acceptable in such cases I quote from a writer in the "Times of India" who was a personal witness in a case of snake-bite and whose account of the modus operandi of "Snake Doctors" is interesting.

"A few days ago, a man of about 40, while cutting grass behind a house, was bitten by a cobra on the finger; he managed to get to his hut, which was just over a hundred yards off, and tell his relatives what had happened. They called in one of the "Specialists" who happened to live near by. This man, while information was being conveyed to two of his confederates, gave the victim a handful of chillies to eat. The man ate them with great relish and declared they were sweet. This was done just to make sure he was playing no tricks, although the two punctures, just over half an inch apart, caused by the fangs of the snake, could clearly be seen.

The victim was losing the use of his legs when he was tied to the trunk of a Neem tree in a sitting position, with four stout ropes around his chest. Scarcely had this been done when five of the " Mystics " arrived, and without asking any questions, prepared to perform the treatment which was to deliver the man from what appeared to be certain death.

Three of these mysterious snake doctors removed their clothing, all except their dhoties, and each brought a lotah full of water, and took up his position about a yard apart and about four yards from the victim, all facing him while two of the older men sat on either side of him; these were soon joined by a third, and on turning around, behold, all the "Deliverers from death" were to be seen awaiting their turn to perform their merciful treatment.

Having taken up their position, the three men standing in front of the striken one began repeating their formula known only to themselves; this was done under their breath, their lips moving at a tremendous pace but uttering no sound. While this was going on they alternatively threw a handful of water out of their lotahs at the inert being in front of them, who by this time had closed his eyes, and, with his head falling to one side, with saliva running from the mouth. Each time the water touched him, a tremor ran through his whole body.

This went on for about fifteen minutes, while I stood by with discredit written all over my face. Then the unbelievable happened—the man's eyes opened with a glassy, uncanny stare in them, and fixed themselves on each man in turn as he threw the water. One of these water throwers informed me later, that although they used cold water the poisoned man felt it as though it was at boiling point.

Now that the man's eyes had opened wide, the spirit of the snake was supposed to have entered his body and the men sitting on either side of him began asking the snake in the man questions, to which intelligent replies were given, just as though the snake was replying. He was asked his name, but he refused to enlighten the "doctors"; asked his caste met with the same negative reply. Asked why he bit the man, he immediately stated that if the man came there again he would bite him a second time.

After the victim had been harassed with persuasive questions by the three men sitting beside him for about half an hour, the other three men having been continuing their water throwing all this while, the tied man went into a violent fit and accused two of the latter of not repeating the correct secret formula. Immediately two other men took their places; and the two who had been relieved admitted later that they were allowing their minds to wander. The treatment had then to start all over again.

The treatment having continued for over two hours, and the questions asked and re-asked dozens of times, the snake in the man was told that it would have to free this man of its venom.

On refusing, pepper corns and chilli seeds were ground together and passed to one of the men asking the questions, who held the powder near the affected man's eyes and informed him that his eyes would be burnt out if he did not answer the questions and free the man. This caused the man to struggle to such an extent that he was on the point of breaking the strong ropes, when another rope was lashed around him, and enough powdered pepper and chilli seeds to cover a rupee were put into one of his eyes. He immediately subsided, and promised to answer all the questions, and to free the man from the poison. But the promise was not sufficient for the "Mystery men," who made him take an oath that he would never bite this man again.

The questions then put to the snake in the man, and his replies were as follows:—

What is your name?—Rama.

Your caste?—A Bhil.

Where do you live?—In a hole under a Peepul tree on the bund of a lake about two hundred yards off.

What do you want?—Tobacco.

Whereupon the man was given a smoke, and some tobacco was also placed under the tree mentioned, (the snake being left to make its own arrangements with regard to a light, if it wanted to smoke it!)

Then he was asked:—

Why did you bite this man?—He was cutting

grass very near where I was lying and his sickle hit me on the back; I was afraid that he would kill me, so I reminded him of my presence.

The water throwers then threw the water along the ground at the side of the man in the direction in which the snake said it lived. The ropes were then removed from the man who walked to his hut, and, after satisfying a somewhat ravenous appetite, had a good night's sleep. Next morning I asked how and where the man was, and was casually told that he was quite fit, and at that moment was trying to blow himself through a big brass musical instrument, for he is a member of the State band, and was at band practice.

Questioned about the previous evening's proceedings, the fortunate man swears that he was bitten by a huge black cobra, while cutting grass, and that after telling his relatives he went into a sound sleep and woke up to have his food about three hours later. The only effect the snake bite left on the man the next day was that his hand felt stiff.

The eye into which the pepper and chillies were put was perfectly normal. This in itself is enough to make the most cynical of us wonder. When I showed astonishment at this and very closely examined the eye the "snake doctors" were very surprised at my foolishness and stated that the snake that bit the man was now perfectly blind in one eye, and why should the man's eye be affected?"

CHAPTER VIII.

DEVIL WORSHIP.

India offers some of the most extraordinary and at the same time concrete examples of demonolatry. Devil worshippers must not be confused with animists, idolaters, or those sects who practise the worship of serpents. On account of its symbolic similitude this is often the case with the last named sect, but these people are in no sense demon worshippers, in-as-much as they propitiate a divine being whose symbol is the snake.

In practice the guiding principle of demonolatry is simplicity itself. God is good, therefore he can do no harm and to worship him is simply a waste of time. The Devil on the other hand is essentially evil and it is well worth while propitiating him and so securing immunity from sickness, poverty and misfortune. On the surface this reasoning leads one to believe that Demon Worship is nothing so very dreadful as it is reputed but in actuality the worship of the evil principle involves such revolting sacrifices and practices that such organisations are a menace to the country and their extermination is highly desirable.

Devil Worship appears to have existed in India from the earliest times. A parable exists in the form of demonolatry practice in Kurdistan from which the Indian variety probably took its source. Sir Richard Temple, C.B.C.I.E., the eminent folklorist and anthropologist has dealt with this subject extensively, and as his remarks throw much light on the origin of this peculiar belief, I quote his observations in full.

To the West of Persia, and generally to the North of Irak or Mesopotamia, there lies a vast mountainous region between the Caspian, Black and Aegean Seas, from Aleppo to Baghdad, covering roughly a great part of Asia Minor, Syria and Palestine, and in this region there have existed in pockets a number of tribes now known collectively as the Kurds. They have been mostly of the fighting class and have consequently played a notable part in history, but their chief service to mankind has been the spreading of religious ideas acquired from the more stable peoples about them from the earliest times. They have been, in fact, a connecting link, as it were, between warring civilisations and beliefs.

Their beginnings are to be found in the ancient Jewish and Babylonian days and they have been subjected to the imperial raids of the Greek Alexander, which once had so overwhelming an effect on the whole of Western Asia, and to the subsequent clash of Parthian and Persian with Greek and Roman. They have imbibed in consequence, through the ages, beliefs of various and even antagonistic descriptions—Babylonian, Assyrian, Zoroastrian, Jewish, early Christian, Greek and Roman. Finally, they succumbed to the all-pervading influence of Islam and are now usually classed as followers of Muhammad (it must be confessed in a most heterodox fashion) and into their Islamic faith they have thrust scraps of, perhaps, every other religion that has crossed their path.

Thus they have come to worship God under the Arabic title of Allah and also under the Persian title of Khuda, the Lord, and various other gods of their own besides, including the Devil, both under his Muhammadan Arabic title of Shaitan or Satan, and other names. Among some of the Kurdish tribes the Devil occupies so prominent a place in the cult, that they have been called by Europeans "Devil-Worshippers."

This requires a little explanation. The terms Devil and Devil-Worshippers do not necessarily denote facts, for they arose in this way. The earliest Europeans and Christian missionaries to the East called every conception of God that was not Jewish, Christian or Muslim, by the deliberately opprobrious name of the Devil and every form of religion other than the three above-mentioned, Devil-Worship.

Thus, to them all the Hindu gods were devils and all the Hindus devil-worshippers. The same terms were applied to Zoroastrians and to all religious sects they came across that paid respect to any being or god that was not of their own kind.

Among the Kurds were several sects that were extremists—Ghulat as the Muslims call them—and of these sects, that which has come most prominently to European notice of late has been the Yezidis who occupy the hilly country to the West of Mosul, a prominent town in Irak on the Tigris and close to the ruins of Nineveh, the ancient capital of the Assyrians.

The Yezidis are a harmless community of Kurds, who keep to their mountain fastnesses and adhere strictly to aboriginal beliefs which are entirely at variance with the Islam they have found it prudent to profess openly owing to the situation of their country. They have chosen a title unfortunate for themselves, as it means that they are ostensibly followers of Yezid, one of the early Muslim Caliphs, and it happens that the name of this hero is anathema to the Shia division of the Muhammadans by whom they are surrounded. The mere fact that they call themselves Yezidis has brought down on them endless, persistent and fanatical persecution through many centuries.

One result of this long-continued ill-treatment has been to make them stick obstinately to the more or less secret objects of their belief, and to convert them into a "peculiar" people.

The Yezidi, as already said, is ostensibly a Muslim, but he is also a true Ghaliya (the Arabic singular of Ghulat), or Extremist, since he believes in many things that are entirely antagonistic to Musilm belief. Thus, he believes in God, i.e., the Arabic Allah whom he also calls by the Persian title of Khuda, the Lord, and also in other deities, i.e., gods or godlings, some ancient and some modern. His eponym, Yezid, is looked upon as a god and so is the reputed founder of his sect, Shekh Adi.

This last was a medieval Shia mystic of a type not at all uncommon in the East, who propounded to the Kurdish tribe, which afterwards became the Yezidis, a sectarian faith of extreme variety, bringing into it a number of ancient pre-Islamic and even pagan ideas. After his death he was defied like Yezid, as one of the gods of the Yezidis who have besides several others, some mythical personages and some even historical in the Mesopotamian region.

The position of these gods is always vague and is much that of the godling or mythical hero among uneducated Hindus or of the saints in some forms of Christianity and Islam. It is right to worship God who is supreme, but it is wise to stand well with the godling, hero or saint who can do infinite harm if neglected—a common attitude in religion all the world over.

But the reason that the Yezidis have been called Devil-worshippers par excellence, in the attention they pay to the Devil—Shaitan or Satan as the Muslims call him. Among them, the greatest power over mankind is that wielded by Allah, or rather Khuda, God, but the opposing power of Shaitan, the Devil, is almost as great—at any rate, in their eyes the power of God is remote, while that of the Devil is imminent and greater than that of Shekh Adi, Yezid, or any other godling.

Therefore, it is most important to the Yezidi to pay attention to the Devil. The feeling may be explained by a story from India. An important Muslim leader in the Punjab was asked why, as a Muslim and believer in Allah, he offered so much service to Guga, the local Hindu Snake-god. He replied that Allah is very remote and an answer to prayer to him both slow and uncertain, whereas Guga is always there and he did not wish to be bitten by a poisonous snake if he neglected him.

There is among the Yezidis an over-powering fear of the Devil; so great, indeed, that he must never be mentioned or even alluded to by name, and many words containing the Arabic letters or sounds of his name (Shaitan), even remotely, are not used. This gives the language a peculiar form owing to the substitutes used for common words—a phenomenon observed elsewhere in the world when common words become "taboo" for ritual reasons. Another consequence has been the concoction of a substitute name, Malik Ta'us, the Lord Peacock (ta'us), or as the Yezidis insist in translating—the Angel Peacock.

Malik Ta'us is and is not an Angel, in a manner common to many sectarian beliefs in the world. He is often quite the equal of Allah and certainly superior to any of the minor Yezidi gods. He is in fact the substitute for Shaitan as the Devil, but despite the antagonism of this idea to orthodox Islam, here is a considerable admixture of Islamic legend in the tales about him, in true Asiatic fashion. Moreover, all the known images of him as a peacock are modern, a fact which goes to show that the cult of Shaitan as Malik Ta'us is modern also.

DEVIL WORSHIP IN THE HIMALAYAS.

I suppose in no country and in the midst of no other civilization has the art of demonolatry been brought to such perfection as in the Himalayas; indeed, it is difficult to make an exception of any one of the Himalayan States, for every one of them is affected.

Demonolatry was in existence in Tibet, Sikkim and Bhutan before the advent of Buddhism and was known as Bhun worship and, although the faith of Tibet and these other States are said to be Buddhism, it is of a form which is not consistent with the teachings of the Lord Buddha or the form of worship practised in the southern countries of Ceylon, Burma and Siam. Buddhism seems to have been tolerant of Bhun worship and, although it has in a great measure replaced it, it has never wholly eradicated this form of demonolatry, but has permitted it to become intermingled with it, until its original form is hardly recognisable. The Mahayana school of thought may be confined in its purity to the monasteries, for what one sees every-day practised by itinerant lamas, is very far removed; and for which Colonel Wadell found a name in 'Lamaism.'

The origin of the Tibetans is lost. They are said to be nomad shepherds from the Mongolian steppes, who on wandering south found vast un-peopled plains with scarce but good pasturage for their flocks and settled in the land.

Demons receive their birth in the imagination of men and fear gives them grotesque and fearful shapes, and these vast plains uninhabited and stretching for miles on either side, as far as the eye can see, worked on the imagination and fear of these nomads, who peopled them with malignant demons which brought into being the exorciser

(Bonting) who waxed fat in body and purse by playing up to the fear of the people.

In Sikkim, it is recognised that the land was a part of Bhot (Tibet) and that the Lepchas are not the original inhabitants but are said to have come in from the East and probably from Assam; a supposition, which, when taking into consideration their habits and customs that on comparison with the tribes of north Assam appear in every respect to be the same, appears to be correct. These Lepchas brought with them many forms of demonolatry from the east, which added to those already in existence in Sikkim, has peopled this State more than any other of the Himalayan States with the worst demons that man's mind could fashion.

Bhutan has always been on a line with Tibet and even today there is no difference in the worship of the two countries.

In Nepal or to be more correct, among the Nepalese, demonolatry reaches a great height of perfection and the profession of the *dhami* or exorciser has become a very lucrative one; the profession can be followed by all castes with the exception of the Brahmin. The calling is said to number many imposters in its ranks, but the man who is believed in and can be relied on, is a much respected person, whose services are sought for on all and frequent occasions and the fees demanded are in proportion to the social status of the client.

I do not write from hearsay, but write of what I have seen with my eyes and witnessed, off and on throughout the year. I once lived in a part of Darjeeling much given to demonolatry and many a night's sleep was lost in consequence of the noise of drumming, of cymbals and conversations with the Evil One, considered necessary to a successful propitiation. The hour of midnight is considered the most suitable, for the world is asleep and quietness reigns over the land and there is no one to disturb your communion with His Satanic Majesty.

The Nepalese have a day set apart in August to the worship of Satan, whom the *dhamis* openly acknowledge as their *Guru* or master. To such an extent has this devil worship got a hold of the people that no occasion is lost for a *puja.* Every occasion, every extraordinary event, is put down as the work of the evil one and immediate necessity arises for propitiation. Sickness, accidents or misfortunes are all signs of his displeasure; and to such an extent has superstition become intermingled with the daily lives of these people, that He, who made these mighty mountains, is only worshipped when all remedies have failed to propitiate the evil one.

The chief shrine of demonolatry among the Tibetans in Darjeeling is the *Kagjhora* (Ravens' Stream), where *Kag,* the mighty demon has his abode. Here lengthy streamers, bearing multi-coloured flags, colours that are representative of the *lokas* or heavens of Buddhism, are stretched from one end to the other, while on every tree may be seen paper prayer flags with the mystic, "Om mani padmi hum" stamped on them, fluttering from the branches to counteract the influence of the evil one, who is said to dwell where the two streams meet. This stream is seldom devoid of a cold breeze and it is possible that this phenomenon has credited the stream as the abode of several demons. Very few lamas pass it without obeisance.

Apart from the devil worship that is now an admixture of Buddhism and has rightly been termed Lamaism, there are peculiar beliefs among the Nepalese of all castes, both high and low, which give the *jhakris*, another word for exorcisers, such a grip on the people. Among these people, the rainbow, one of the finest sights to be seen during the monsoon, is said to be the devil drinking his fill from some hill stream, clothed in all the bright colours so that his nearness to the world appears pleasant and in this way lures many unsuspecting children to their doom.

Much could be written on the various forms of demonolatry, but for brevity only one instance is taken to show to what depth the people have sunk.

The Nepali, with all his cheerfulness is a vindicative individual, the women more so than the men. They are capable of nursing their grievances for months and leave it to time to furnish them with an opportunity for revenge.

I have known cases where one woman has put the 'flue' on another and the victim of this diabolical revenge has suffered the pangs of hell, because of her belief in black magic which is sheer fright, pure and simple. When cases of this sort occur and the victim has been able to trace the perpetrator, it is imperative for her to engage the services of a *dhami* or *Jhakri* to counteract the influence and throw it back on the perpetrator. Cowardice is not a trait of the Nepali's character, but in these cases the victims are reduced to an abject state of terror and remain in this state, until the particular *Jakhri* they have faith in, can be procured to render the 'flue' abortive. These *pujas* run the people into debt and they sell their jewellery or get into the clutches of some rapacious *bania.*

It will be curious to know how the 'flue' can be made to act. Every movement of the victim of a person's revenge is carefully watched and no opportunity lost to get the wherewithal to propitiate the evil one to cast the 'flue'. Should he or she go for a walk, the dust from the indentation made by the heel of the shoe is gathered and offered. A fragment torn from the clothes worn by a victim, if obtainable, is placed in a bamboo tube which is rubbed with vermillion and planted near a stream to obtain the desired revenge. But the most efficacious offering is a hair from the head of the victim, treated in a similar way as the torn fragment of her clothes.

Pregnant women are considered fair game by those who are not similarly blessed. It may be they do not know one another, but still that one should be blessed and the other not, is sufficient to rouse the inordinate jealously which is inherent in all Nepalese.

On all festive occasions, whether puja or sport, the aim of the wealthy classes is to adorn themselves in rich silks, satins, jewellery and shawls, to excite the envy of their more unfortunate sisters. The Nepalese, moreover, are adepts in the art of raising a quarrel, and this they do by wounding the feelings of those they imagine are attempting to excite their envy; but not in a direct way, but in a very indirect manner by passing remarks verging on insults about some third person similarly adorned. And if the persons they really intend to insult should take it upon themselves to resent the remarks, this is sufficient to form the basis of a long quarrel, which may extend to years, eventually ending in exorcising and counteracting the 'flue,' and much money is spent in this way. Incidently, and in every case, the *dhami* is the richer by the transaction and, although he may not foster these quarrels, it is to his advantage to see that it lasts long, for the longer it lasts the richer the harvest he reaps.

CASTING OUT DEVILS.

Naturally the growth and development of such a cult has led to a host of crime associated with its beliefs and practices. The Hindus in particular are adepts at casting out devils and I give the account of an eye-witness explaining how this is done.

One may live a long time in India, especially in the large cities and towns, without witnessing a real exhibition of the power of the devil over those evil spirits that are supposed to get certain individuals in their grip.

That the devil priest is in considerable demand one instinctively feels in this land, but unless one is acquainted with the inner workings of Indian religious practices it is easy to miss the opportunity of witnessing the interesting, and to most of us, disgusting rites that are performed.

During a recent visit to Poona the writer, attracted by a motley crowd of men and women, led by three or four men, dressed in the most weird costumes, saw some part, at least, of the performance, for in all probability other rites had been carried out in the secrecy of the house before the procession left. That it was not an ordinary crowd making its way to the riverside near the Sangam, to carry out the ordinary rites of their faith, was evident as soon as one approached. Supported by men, one could distinguish in the crowd four or more women who were evidently in a drugged state for without support it was quite impossible for them to move a step.

As the procession approached the river the devil priests who were leading, demanded that a passage should be made, and the drugged women were placed in a line. At the order from the devil priest, the women were forced to make an attempt to run toward the priests, who were waiting with open arms to hold them. Not one of them was able to run so far, but tumbled down, one or two very heavily, on the rough ground.

The crowd raised them up and the devil priests began to practise their art on them one by one. They rubbed their arms, they touched their eyes, they poured stuff down their throats, they passed their hands before their faces, and after a while several of them showed signs of coming to their senses, but one refused to respond to all the efforts of the devil priests, and lay in a pitiful state on the ground, her face an ashen white.

Meanwhile, those who had recovered from

what were clearly the effects of some strong drug were led to the river, and further efforts to restore the obstinate one were made. The leader now seated himself beside the river, and drew from his bag a variety of materials, all of some magic significance, and began to mix them.

Then came the final part of the ceremony. A cock was brought. Its head was quickly decapitated, and after pronouncing certain magic formulae, it was thrown into the river, by which act doubtless the evil spirits which had laid hold on the women, were consigned to the deep. In the meantime, the obstinate one appeared to have shown a distinct change, and no longer did she have that appearance of unconsciousness on her face.

One wonders what share the writer had in this, for as soon as the crowd turned their attention to the photographer, and left off their ministrations, she quickly recovered.

The foregoing explains the *modus operandi* of the exorciser and shows the extraordinary hold these people have on the minds and imaginations of their unfortunate followers, but there is another aspect of the question, that relating to extortion. Since all ills, disease and suffering are due to satanic influence, these people are ever ready, for a consideration, to drive out the evil spirit and so cure the disease or alleviate the suffering. I will quote one instance which shows how these people work. The case is from the Sub-Divisional Magistrate Court at Alipore and reads as follows:—

Babu Srish Chandra Sinha, Pleader moved a very queer petition on behalf on one Kalipada Patra of Belpukur P.S., Matiabruz, against Jogesh Chatterjee and 5 others for having abducted the wife of the complainant named Charubala Dasee under very peculiar circumstances.

The prosecution case is that the complainant suffered from various diseases for about a year and and taking advantage of his physical and mental condition the accused gave out to the relations of the complainant who are also accused in this case that the complainant is possessed by an evil spirit which is undermining his body and mind, and that he alone as a charmer could cure him. Having thus introduced himself into the family he gradually won over the whole family and at last was successful in luring the wife of the complainant. The accused have now all left the house of the complainant after taking away the wife and all the life's savings of the complainant amounting to Rs. 3,000. The man is now in a wretched state of body, mind and purse.

The Magistrate ordered the issue of warrant against Jogesh and also ordered a search warrant for the production of the girl in Court.

CHAPTER IX.

HAUNTS AND SCHOOLS OF CRIME.

I will make no attempt to discuss this subject in its entirety. The question of motives, of criminal characteristics and repressive measures, although interesting, can find no place in a work of this type. There is however a class of crime, which on account of its bearing directly and indirectly on the subject of night haunts, of opium dens and gambling saloons, should be described. I will deal with them generally under the heads,—Pickpockets, Thefts and Confidence Tricks.

Of the first I have very little to say. This amiable fraternity is too well known to need any detailed description, but their cleverness and the time and practice, devoted to securing a proficiency in this light-fingered art is surely worthy of a better cause. Pickpockets are as numerous in the streets of Calcutta and in the majority of Eastern Cities as in London. They work best where traffic is congested—in crowded buses and tram-cars and seem to reap quite a good harvest at the entrances to Cinema Shows and Theatres.

I once had a note-book robbed from the breast-pocket of my coat. This note-book used to contain every class of notes except those issued by the local currency office and was quite a bulky affair. How and when it was taken I have not the faintest idea and yet I could have sworn that the removal of such a bulky package from my breast-pocket, without my knowledge, was impossible. Some idea of its size may be judged from the fact that several of my well-intentioned friends referred to this same pocket-book as my "Hunch-producing apparatus" declaring that every time I took it out for reference they got the "hunch" and when I put it back I had a tendency to become hunch-backed myself. And yet this book was removed from my pocket without difficulty apparently and absolutely without my knowledge. Well, all I can say is—"bravo."

CRIMINAL METHODS DESCRIBED.

Of thieves and the ways of thieves I am diffident. I know quite a lot about these folk, but the more I see of them and study their methods the more convinced am I that these people work in cliques, directed probably by a master mind. However, there is one point that must be emphasized and that is the improvement in methods, the "modern touch" in present-day robberies. That thieving to-day is becoming a profession highly organised and perfectly equipped is apparent to the most casual observer. The old, crude methods of thieving are fast disappearing. "Gentlemen Burglars" are becoming sufficiently numerous to deprive this type of many of their romantic features. The "gentleman" who relieves you of your superfluous cash, does so in such an accomplished way that he leaves you guessing quite awhile. But one old type still survives and of this type I deal principally. He is the scoundrel who divests himself of all clothing, who oils and greases his body till he becomes as slippery as an eel and at dead of night creeps in through the open window, collects your collar-studs and cuff-links with a fine discrimination for genuine and counterfeit, opens your almirah with keys, previously supplied by obliging domestics and makes off with your finest suits and the latest thing in shirts and ties.

It is this class of thief that is a god-send to the second-hand dealer. He represents stock, both actual and potential, and is encouraged in his nefarious trade till the long arm of the Law collects him within the fold.

I now come to the most interesting phrase—from a psychological standpoint—of this lucrative profession. Indians are universally credited with a large amount of natural shrewdness, but in the hands of a capable "confidence agent" they seem as simple as children.

Watch with me that venerable Yogi proceeding down the street, nude, save for a loin cloth and a few ashes, and bearing in his hand the dried half of a large cocoanut shell. He halts for a moment before the door of a wealthy zemindar. His profession and sanctity are a sufficient passport and he enters the house unopposed. In the quadrangle within (all purely Eastern houses are built on the quadrangular principle, the living rooms on the three sides face the main entrance, the space in the middle being used for a reception court, bathing platform, etc.) he raises his voice in some ancient Sanskrit slogan. A female head appears at one of the heavily-barred windows and a pice falls in the

Yogi's bowl. The recipient looks up and smiles and while thanking her rattles his bowl and lo! the one pice has turned into two. The female head disappears and in a moment three heads re-appear and three pice fall to the ground. The Yogi condescendingly picks them up, places them in his bowl and invoking the name of God passes his hand over the bowl. The miracle is repeated—in place of the three pice there are now six. There is a cry of surprise and again the three heads disappear from the window. A little later a door leading into the quadrangle opens cautiously and a female figure beckons to the Yogi. Entering, he is immediately surrounded by a bevy of heavy-eyed, olive-skinned Eastern beauties, clad in the flimsiest of material. One produces a rupee. "Can the Holy man duplicate this?" The Holy man condescends. The rupee is laid in the empty bowl. The bowl is covered with a dirty piece of cloth. Two lean brown hands make mysterious passes, the cloth is removed and there—two rupees where there should only be one. The Yogi solemnly returns the rupee to the owner; he then blesses them reverently and departs saying he will come again.

Three days later he returns. Again the same miracles are performed, but this time the Yogi gives a little advice.

"My daughters, you have been kind to an old man. Come now, I will shew you how in a few moments you may become rich beyond your dreams. Bring me your jewels, your diamonds, your rubies, your pearls. Lay them in this magic bowl and all you place herein shall be doubled." There is a flutter and much racing and tittering and soon the heavy-eyed beauties return laden with jewels, with family heirlooms and old gold mohurs. These are all poured into the magic bowl and covered. But the ritual is now changed. Instead of the old rag, the Yogi unwinds a large shawl from his shoulders with which he covers both himself and the jewels. After awhile he emerges muttering several Sanskrit slogans and then asks for "ganga-jal," the sacred water of the Ganges. This is not forthcoming Then he must get some. If it is forthcoming, it is not fresh and fresh water is essential. Bidding the women watch by the shawl and warning them on no account to raise it, the Yogi departs to fetch the sacred water.

The women watch and wait patiently. The morning wears on to noon and noon to evening, but still the Yogi does not return. With darkness come the men of the house back from work. They are told of the miracle. The shawl is rudely cast aside and below is found an empty bowl. The saintly Yogi is never seen in that locality again.

This is one phrase of the confidence trick, another is known as "Note Duplicating." This trick is usually worked on rustic labourers coming to the city to deposit their hard earned savings in the Government Savings Banks. When such a rustic is located by a "Note Duplicating" sharper, he usually proceeds to gain his confidence by duplicating smaller coins. He obtains a four anna bit from the rustic, applies some acid, strikes it sharply with a knife and returns two four anna bits to the astonished country man. This goes on till coins of a high value are reached and the labourer is convinced of the genuineness of the trick. He is then induced to part with all his earnings. Sharpers of this type usually carry two bags identical in appearance. In one is placed some old coins and pieces of paper; the other is empty. As soon as the labourer hands over his money this is put into the empty bag. The sharper then at the first favourable opportunity exchanges the two. Giving his victim the wrong bag to hold he tells him that he must get some more acid to complete the duplication of all this money. In this way he makes a good "get-away" and it is usually some time before the labourer, growing suspicious at his protracted absence, opens the bag and discovers that he has been duped. There is one other form of deception, which because of its very ingenuity I mention. This cannot be classed as a "confidence trick" it is rather a supreme test of honesty.

Two Anglo-Indian lads, well dressed and seemingly respectable, were once observed walking down one of the main thoroughfares of the city. Keeping at a respectable distance from each other, the first lad in drawing his handkerchief from his pocket dropped accidently, it seemed, a purse from his pocket. A passerby on the same pavement noticing the purse fall picked it up and calling to the lad returned it to him. The boy thanked the gentleman and the two parted. The same lad had not gone another five hundred yards when again his purse fell to the pavement seemingly unobserved. In the second instance it was picked up by a gentleman whose moral susceptibilities were not as fine as that of his predecessor. Seeing that the purse was well filled and that he was unobserved he quietly pocketed his find, making off down a quiet lane. It was now time for the second lad to act. In a moment he was after the culprit whom he stopped and demanded to know what he had found. Indignantly this unfortunate gentleman denied having found anything. At this moment the first lad returned, looking anxiously on the ground for his lost purse. The second lad called to him informing him that the gentleman had his purse. This was again denied and the first lad, thereupon, offered to call the police and have the gentleman searched. Realizing the awkward predicament he was in the gentleman now offered to return the purse, but his offer was indignantly refused. Both boys were for calling the police and their victim realizing how he had compromised himself was equally anxious to keep out of the clutches of the Law.

The result is, of course, obvious. As a last resource the gentleman offers to compensate the first lad for the annoyance caused him and a sum of Rs. 50, technically as compensation and actually as hush money, is paid over. The game is then repeated and quite a fortune made. In this way honesty has its reward, greed is punished, and two scoundrels flourish at the expense of their neighbour's weakness.

In conclusion, I will quote from the "Statesman" of the 4th November 1928 an interesting account of wholesale swindling and the methods adopted. This account describes the famous "Bead Game" by which so many unsuspecting persons have been duped.

"A sensational story of systematic swindling by a band of young men—some of whom belong to families of high standing in Indian society in Calcutta—was told yesterday by Mr. N. N. Banerji, the Public Prosecutor, before Mr. N. R. Mookherji, Special Magistrate at Alipore, when Bhupendranath Sarkar and 21 others were charged with being members of a gang who entered into a criminal conspiracy to defraud the public by novel devices.

The Public Prosecutor made a number of serious allegations against the accused, who, he said, defrauded their known victims of over one lakh of rupees. Nearly forty cases of swindling by the gang had been discovered up to now. About 200 witnesses are to be examined for the prosecution.

"This gang," said Mr. Banerji, "is a cosmopolitan group of persons hailing from Bengal, Bihar, Orissa and the U. P., composed of both Hindus and Mohammedans drawn from every stratum of society from a zemindar's son—a scion of the Sovabazar Raj family—to an orderly or durwan. "Bhupen Sarkar," the Public Prosecutor added, "is the brain of this conspiracy and the leader of the gang." Sarkar comes of a zemindar family of Peasara, a village near Tarakeswar. A couple of years ago he lived in a small rented house at Durgacharan Banerjee Road in Calcutta.

"In 1926 Sarkar conceived the idea of starting a 'swindling den' and with this end in view he took a lease of a luxuriously furnished garden house at Dum Dum called Rose Villa, on a monthly rent of Rs. 500. Two of the accused named Gokulananda Patra and Baidhar Puley, who were formerly servants in the garden house, were taken into confidence by Bhupen. Gradually other members joined and about six of them came to live permanently in the house.

"The *modus operandi* of this gang," continued Mr. Banerji, "was to lure unwary people into the garden house by holding up before them magnificent prospects of business transactions resulting in a certain and speedy acquisition of wealth. Several emissaries were at work to find out suitable victims in Calcutta and also in the mofussil. The usual story to the victims was that in the garden house there lived an immensely rich man, who did not know what to do with his wealth and wanted to invest his money in business or in endowments for charitable and philanthropic institutions.

"To a struggling physician the bait was that the rich man wanted to open a hospital and charitable dispensary on a big scale in memory of his deceased mother and he (the doctor) might be placed in charge of that institution on a handsome salary, free quarters with permission to take up outside practice. To the owner of a declining rice mill the representation would be that the rich master of the emissary desired to start a rice mill on a big scale and might utilise the service of the owner for a start. To a dealer in jute in a remote village at Midnapur the story would be told that the rich man would supply capital for a jute business to be opened in partnership with the dealer.

" A building contractor on the look out for work would be told that a princely mansion would be built for which his service would be required. To a dealer in elephants the story would be that the rich man would purchase half a dozen tuskers from the wilds of distant Mayurbhunj.

" By such blandishments, and many others, the vistims were decoyed to the garden house and introduced to one of the members as Manager. This man would speak in glowing terms of the prospects of substantial gain and would gradually throw out a suggestion that the victim would have to provide some money as security or advance or as *dasturi*. Invariably the victim would not get audience of the rich man on the first day. This would impress upon him the importance of the person.

" On the second day the victim would be introduced to the Babu, who would leave everything to be settled by the Manager. Subsequently, when the victim would come with some money, the Babu would come and the money would be placed before or handed over to the Manager. Just at this moment another member of the gang would arrive dramatically carrying information about the mortgage or sale of a very big property valued at several lakhs of rupees.

"When about to leave, after obtaining instructions from the Babu, the man would suddenly turn round and show the Babu a novel game in beads and induce the Babu to play with him on a wager and in a few minutes, in the presence of the victim, he would gain a thousand rupees or thereabout from the Babu who would at once pay down the sum.

"The victim would be coaxed to join the game and the money of the victim, brought for the purpose of business, and the Manager's contribution would be mixed up and the Manager would explain to the victim how by a contrivance they would never lose. Even if the victim was unwilling the Babu would be sent for and the Manager would play, on behalf of the victim, with the Babu and by a dishonest manipulation of the beads bring about a heavy loss for the victim.

"The Babu would then remove the money and would force the victim to execute a hand note for the balance and some documents to indicate that he had on his own accord entered into the game. The victim would then be driven off with a threat that if he informed the police his life would be in danger. A quarter of the money thus realised from the victim would at once be divided and the balance kept for a week and if the victim instituted a case or kicked up a fuss, the matter would be settled by a refund of a portion of the amount, otherwise the balance would again be divided."

CHAPTER X.

CHORE HAT OR THIEVES' MARKET.

There is in Calcutta a relic of a time reminiscent of thuggism, an old market place known as "Chore Hat"—"the Thieves' Market."

This unsavoury reputation is well deserved, but there are indications that originally this market started on very different lines. About 25 to 30 years ago a wealthy and patriotic Indian conceived the idea of building a market under his own name which would cater for the residents of the locality now known as Bow Bazar. Consequently he built a small market consisting of a number of detached booths, clustered together in a small square, and called it "Kali Das Seal's Market." Five years later the appearance of this market had greatly altered. The fruit, vegetable and meat vendors had all disappeared and in their place had come a number of second-hand dealers (bekris) who did a flourishing trade in old boots, hats, clothes, etc., and from them originated the name "Purana Hat" or "Second-hand Market." As may be expected such a market attracted a large number of traders of a sinister type. Receivers of stolen property, thieves and swindlers, money coiners and the like all came here to barter their goods and gradually the market came to be known as "Chore Hat" or "the Thieves' Market."

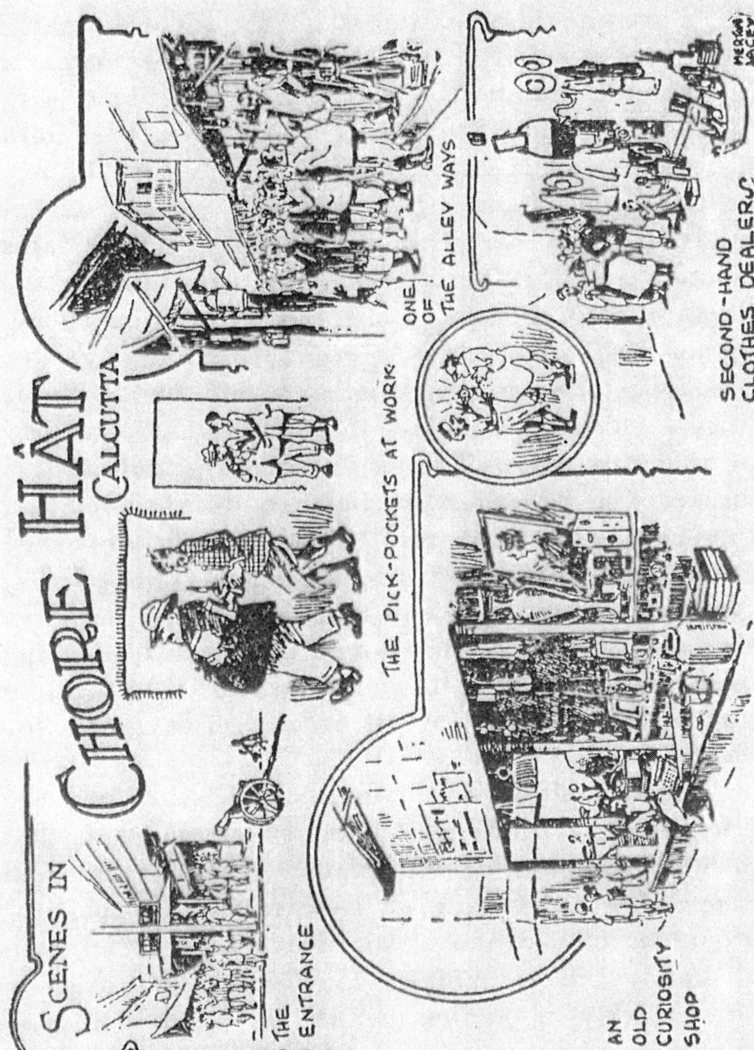
SCENES IN CHORE HÂT CALCUTTA
THE ENTRANCE
THE PICK-POCKETS AT WORK
ONE OF THE ALLEY WAYS
AN OLD CURIOSITY SHOP
SECOND-HAND CLOTHES DEALERS

I recommend anyone interested in old landmarks of Calcutta to pay a visit to this place. To the newcomer its location is one of some difficulty. The market itself is not visible from the road. It lies about a hundred yards west of the junction of Wellington and Bow Bazar Streets on the right hand side and is entered by a narrow lane known as Gourdea's Lane. The market, true to its reputation, opens only at night. All day it remains closed, practically deserted, but the instant the lights are lit, booths, stalls, and platforms spring up as if by magic. A seething jostling mass of humanity pour in and the scramble for bargains begins. What a medley of goods, what a display of ancient finery. Things our great grandmothers discarded as too old-fashioned are still displayed on the heaped up counters. Bric-a-brac of every description. Clothes, boots, hats, gramophones, cameras. Anything and everything and at prices that stagger you. Things you could not buy in the open market for Rs. 10 going for Re. 1 and others you would not buy at all at any price going for Rs. 10.

But the sights and sounds of "Chore Hat" are not its sole attractions. There is ever present that peculiar element of uncertainty, that "what will happen next?" feeling. "Beware of Pickpockets" would be idle advice in this place. The thief who so kindly relieves you of your superfluous cash in so masterly a manner would be insulted if you designated him as an ordinary pickpocket. He is in fact a trained professional, a master of his art and a member of a very lucrative profession. To cite an instance, I had purchased a pair of brand new tan shoes for Rs. 5. With jealous care I watched the shopkeeper pack these treasures away in a card-board box and tie it round with a piece of twine. Taking the box firmly under my arm I pushed my way through the crowd till I came to where a number of second-hand cameras attracted my attention. Here I entered into a lengthy debate with the old rogue who tried to palm on me a very fair imitation of the "Camera Obscura" and refused to be convinced when I tried to explain that a camera minus the shutter and lens was of no use to anybody. At length exhausted with the impossible task of trying to make him understand I left in disgust and returned home consoled with the thought that I had at least made one bargain. Eager to view my purchase I undid the twine, snatched off the cover and discovered—nothing. For a few minutes I saw red. But after a while I calmed down and proceeded to examine the box only to find that one end had been cut out, the shoes extracted and the card-board replaced. Even the twine was intact.

Like Boadecia of old I rushed back next evening. Without a moment's hesitation I proceeded to the shop from which I had purchased the shoes. The shopkeeper met me, all smiling and bland, and then, before I could utter a word, before I could even think of what I wanted to say, he presented me with another pair of tan shoes, assuring me the while that as I had now become a regular customer of his, he would sell me this pair cheap, dust cheap in fact—only Rs. 3. Imagine my condition, my feelings, when I recognised at a glance the very same pair he had sold me the day previous. I confess, such colossal, bare-faced, brazen robbery fills me with a sense of helplessness. Meekly I paid the Rs. 3 and left without a word, but before I went I first wore the new pair, carrying the old openly in my hands.

There is, however, one honest man in this den of iniquity. One evening while prowling round this unsavoury locality my eye was suddenly arrested by a red sign-board, on which appeared the wholly unexpected phrase "Prices Fixed." I had never thought such a thing possible in Chore Hat, so advancing towards the counter I picked up a new electric switch.

"How much?" I asked. The boy attending the counter disappeared within and a moment later an old Mohammedan appeared. "Twelve anna" he said and pointed smiling to the sign above.

I could have dropped. Imagine being asked the correct price of anything in Chore Hat.

"Here" thought I "is a man whose acquaintance should be cultivated" and thereafter I made it a practice of visiting his shop at frequent intervals, till I soon became known to this honest old Islamite and from him learned many things about the underworld of the great cities of the East. I remember once mentioning my loss of the tan shoes and commenting on the skill with which they had been removed. The old man smiled indulgently at my lack of experience and then told me the following strange tale of the ways of thieves in India.

"In my youth," he said, "I was reckoned among the cleverest thieves in Delhi and proud I was of this great distinction. But of course I had a natural aptitude for thieving. My father was a great man before me."

"And now," I ventured, "do you still practise this lucrative profession?"

He spat on the ground disdainfully. "The cursed British Raj. They spoil everything. I was a wealthy man once. Now I work from morn till night and scarcely can I live," and his glance swept contemptuously round his little shop. "But I was telling you of my youth."

"One day when I was but twelve years of age I needed money. Two rupees only, but my father refused to help me. So I waited my opportunity, saw him place some money in a little bag and tie the same in one corner of his *lungi* round his waist. Evening came and my father, like all good Moslems, turning his face to Mecca, bowed himself in prayer. With him I prayed, watching my opportunity and when he lay prostrate, kissing the earth in humility, I took a knife from my girdle and with one swift stroke cut the *lungi* extracting the bag. Undisturbed my father prayed on, but when he had finished he turned to me and laying his hand affectionately on my shoulder blessed me. "Here are the Rs. 2 you require, son," he said. I looked up and saw in his hand the very same bag which a moment before I had extracted from his *lungi*. Wondering greatly, I felt in my pocket for the bag. It was gone. My father smiled at my chagrin, but bade me cheer up, "For a novice, 'twas well done indeed. To-morrow you shall learn more."

"Next morning he took me through many dark lanes and evil smelling alleys right into the heart of Chandni Chowk. Here we stopped before a small wooden door upon which my father knocked thrice in rapid succession. It was opened by an old woman who smiled on seeing my father but frowned at the sight of me. My father, however, whispered something to her and apparently satisfied she bade us follow her. Through ill-lit gloomy passages she conducted us till we came to a large hall in which hung garments of various kinds and other strange contrivances. Here an old man met us. After the usual greeting he enquired the purpose of our visit. "He has talent," said my father, referrnig to me "Let him be tried."

"The old man clapped his hands and a youth appeared. Without a word he handed the boy a rupee, which the lad in turn placed in one of the pockets of the garment nearest to me. 'Now,' whispered my father. "Take that rupee out, but be careful you do not shake the garment as you do it." I smiled contemptuously at the simplicity of the task and deftly thrust my hand into the pocket. The instant, however, my fingers came in contact with that rupee, a thousand hidden bells, attached to the garment, started ringing. Again I tried and again, more cautiously each time, but ever with the same result. At last the old man grew impatient. "Shew him, Ahmed," he cried, and the lad advanced proudly towards me. For an instant his hand seemed to linger near the garment, the next, the self same rupee lay in his open palm. I marvelled greatly, but there came a time when this same Ahmed vied with me in such feats of skill but every time was I proclaimed the winner. Here it was I received my tuition in such noble professions as pick-pocketing, breaking safes, opening locks and manufacturing skeleton keys of every description. For the few years I practised this lucrative profession with my father, we amassed great wealth, and then came my downfall.

"One day, so daring had I become, I entered the bungalow of the Superintendent of Police himself. In a moment his safe lay open and his treasures all but mine, when by some mischance I threw over a vase that stood on a small table near me. The dog of a Ferringee slept lightly. I had all but reached the window when there came a blinding flash, a sharp shooting pain through my right palm and when I reached home, bruised and faint from loss of blood, a look at my hand showed me that my professional career was at an end. Assiduously I trained my left hand, but never was it quite the same as my right, and so perforce I settled down to this miserable trade, striving to earn a living honestly."

The old man relapsed into silence, reminiscent, perhaps, with memories of his lost youth and I rose to go.

"Have a cigarette, Abdul?" I ventured. He nodded and I sought my case. It was gone. Rapidly I searched through every pocket. They were all empty. A terrible suspicion flashed across my mind. "Abdul" I began sternly, but the old man smiled reassuringly. "They are all on the chair behind you, Sahib," he said "you see my hand has not lost its cunning yet."

In silence I pocketed my belongings and left the shop, I was in fact too astonished to speak.

CONFESSIONS OF AN ARCH DACOIT AND PRISON BREAKER.

Reverting now to the question of ordinary thieving and the marked improvements noticed in the methods employed, I give below, as a typical example, the history of a notorious rogue which provides a fine insight into the methods employed by these people and incidently throws some light on those "Schools of Crime" which I have described in the foregoing chapter.

"My Experiments in Burglary" would be a fitting title to the amazing autobiographical sketch which Babu Chasmawalla, the arch dacoit and prison breaker, made before the Bandra Magistrate in Bombay on 16th October, 1926.

With considerable candour he related his many exploits in chronological order.

Beginning as a school teacher, he said, he was sent to prison for embezzlement, and realised his unfitness for Government service in future. At this moment there stepped in an old offender who counselled him to take to thieving. Chasmawalla jumped at the idea and took lessons from his *guru*.

He soon became a master of the art and in order to hoodwink the police he paraded as a wealthy merchant purporting to sell goods of all descriptions which he was supposed to have purchased at auctions. Fashionable European hotels, first class compartments, bunglows and a princely suite formed his method of impressing the world.

He commenced his narrative by saying "I passed my third-year training examination in Mahratti and served as a schoolmaster in Aurangabad District till 1919. In November of that year I was appointed head master of a school in Parbhai District.

"A branch Post Office was attached to the school, where Postal, Bank and Money Order work was carried on in Urdu. While in charge of that work I committed defalcations in the Postal accounts to the tune of Rs. 2,500, for which I was tried and sentenced to three months' imprisonment."

This incident seemed to be the turning point in his life as it hardened him into a professional criminal.

Chasmawalla himself says "I underwent that sentence in Chanchanwada Jail. There was in the same jail a Jewish convict, Lawrence by name, who had been sentenced to six months' for cheating. He had had one or two previous convictions for theft.

"In Jail I was considerably depressed, contemplating as to what I should do in later life.

"As I had become unfit for Government service, Lawrence stepped in as adviser and suggested I should take to thieving. His reasoning appealed to me and I decided what I was going to be in future life. Accordingly I made myself acquainted with all methods of committing thefts, boring walls, breaking open locks, removing rivetted bars from doors and windows, destroying cement work with acid, and opening from outside, doors closed from inside. In all these and other matters I soon acquired proficiency. There were 4,000 to 5,000 fellow prisoners in Chanchanwada Jail, fifty of whom were expert crooks equipped with expert knowledge and endowed with wit and abundant resourcefulness."

A budding thief came out of prison with all the world for his booty and he chose his own town of Aurangabad for his debut.

"After release," he said, "I returned to Aurangabad and began committing thefts and within a month and a half I brought off ten to fifteen.

"During this early period I collected various materials required for house-breaking. I also tried to become a good shot and practised with pistols and guns in the jungle. Violence did not appeal to me and I turned my attention to different methods of action.

"I rented a bungalow in Aurangabad to serve as my headquarters and from there I carried on my thieving activities. I was passing off as a wealthy Mahomedan leather merchant. I had one or two conveyances, a treasury, a signboard, a letter-box, and three or four servants.

"I continued to throw dust in the eyes of the police for some time, but eventually the bubble burst and I was arrested.

"Later, I went to Poona, rented a bungalow and opened a pedhi. I pretended to be grain broker, but after two or three months I was discovered and had to run. I escaped from custody but was recaptured in a train between Kirkee and Chinchwad. Although I was let off by the Bench Magistrate I did not stay in Poona as I became a marked figure there.

"My next choice fell on Surat where I paraded under the name of Javeri, and a victoria driver named Dawood used to take me for a drive every day. He found out my real trade and offered to assist me, and as I always required another man's assistance in my thefts I complied and instructed him in my system of wandering throughout the town, noting big shops, and breaking open closed doors at night without hurting any one.

"In Surat, too, I was found out and sent to jail for three months.

"The mofussil became too tame for me and on my release from prison I wended my way to the Metropolis of the Presidency.

"I had profited by my experiences in the past and had learnt that I was caught not in committing thefts but in disposing of stolen property. This flaw in my armour I repaired during my stay in Bombay. My object was to sell the stolen goods in public with all the appearance of a *bona fide* transaction. With this purpose in view I made friends with leading merchants in the city. I called on them frequently, and asked them to return the visits. I used motor cars freely, entertained them, when they visited me, with gramophones, gave nautch parties in their honour, went with them to theatres, took them on various trips to big cities, lodging in fashionable European hostels, but never gave away my real calling. Thus I had lodged with them in the Taj Mahal Hotel, the London Hotel in Poona, the National and Napier Hotels in Lucknow, the Royal and Wellington Hotels in Lahore, the Wellesley and Cashmere Hotels in Calcutta, the Betty and Mary Hotels in Sholapur, the Maharaja's Hotel and Government Travellers' Bungalow in Gwalior, and a number of others.

"In Kirkee I secured a contract from the military authorities for the supply of grain in order to be able to mention an ostensible profession as a cloak under which I continued to commit thefts in and round about Poona.

"After some time, I again went to Bombay and opened pedhis in Girgaum, Pydhonie, Kalbadevi, Musjid Bundar, and other places.

"In November and December 1924 and January 1925, I committed Rs. 6 lakhs of thefts.

"My next theft was in Thana district, for which I was sent to jail. On the very day of my release I committed another theft. What could I do? I had only 14 annas on me, being the balance with me when I left the jail. The shop from which I stole was located at the Naka, close to the jail. The servant had gone out and the shop was unguarded. I stepped in and stole property worth Rs. 75 and disposed of it at Ghatkopar and Dadar, part by pledging, and part by selling.

"On my return to Bombay, I found my pedhis in a chaos. Dawood Gani had gone with the articles in some of the pedhis. The servants were not there. I did not know what had happened. I entered the Girgaum branch at night by the back door, as the front door was closed, taking some hand-bills and envelopes and some clothing, and went to Virar the same night. There I committed a theft on the railway which put me in funds to the extent of Rs. 1,150.

"With this as my capital I started another campaign.

"I have already said that I always needed an associate. I wanted a literate man, I have often considered that a Gujerati or a Brahman from those parts would be highly suitable. Hindu thieves always congregate in Madhavbag, and from these I selected Pyarilal the second accused as he appeared to be a man without much vice, and one who would carry out my orders.

"I engaged part of a Bungalow at Andheri. My experience has taught me that people in Bombay have ready gold and money, but in the suburban districts they have it in the shape of land or in the bank.

"I had a conviction that in the suburbs I would get more of cloth, silk, etc. Moreover I could not go back to Bombay as every police station displayed my photograph, and every constable knew me—hence my choice of Andheri. If I went towards Bombay at all I went only as far as Parel, and even then I used to spend my time in the trains and in distributing handbills.

"On one such occasion I met Haji, the second accused. I was dressed in complete khaki. Haji asked me whether the notice I was distributing was in respect of Gandhi, or Shaukat Ali. I read out the contents of the notice and explained to him their significance. Its purport was that every kind of gold and silver ornament, cloth and other articles could be had cheaply from us as we obtained them in auctions. We did not consider any offer for goods of the value of less than Rs. 500. Business places and hours were notified in the various branch pedhis in the city of Bombay, and special terms were offered for transactions in the Andheri office. As my business improved I enlarged my furniture and show arrangements at Andheri.

"The stolen goods were stored in an interior room to which no one had access. The central hall began to be visited by all and sundry and I placed newspapers in the hall. The reading room was free to all who chose to call. Railway station masters, pleaders, contractors, traders and citizens patronised the shop. I passed for a big merchant and owned two first class season tickets between Bombay and Virar."

The leader of the gang also gave details of the circumstances in which he came across the other accused in the case and explained how he made tools of them by engaging them as his servants on a liberal remuneration.

Most of them were not, however, in his confidence, Pyarilal and Dawood Gani being the only two in whom he confided all his plans and secrets.

Among the other details revealed by him was the toilette box he carried with him for enabling him to assume the character of a Mahomedan, Hindu, Christian, Sikh or Parsi at will.

The statement also contained a reference to the creed of non-violence uniformly pursued by Chasmawalla, an instance of which was furnished during the raid of a dilapidated house of Babu Khoti Street carried out a few months back by the Bombay police.

"Dawood was ready to kill the head police officer of the raiding party, but I showed him a way out of the difficulty which involved no danger to life, namely, by removing the bars. Inspector Dyer and others chased him, but Dawood fired at a sub-inspector. Had I been there, I would not have allowed him to do so."

Pyarilal practically admitted most of the allegations against him and corroborated Chasmawalla in his statement that the accused numbers 2, 3, 4 and 6 were merely employees of Chasmawalla.

He (Pyarilal) alone used actively to assist Chasmawalla in thefts as well as disposal of property.

The above confession reads like a romance, but when it is confirmed by over 152 prosecution witnesses its authenticity can no longer be doubted. Discussing modern methods in crime with a Police officer, who is a recipient of the King's medal, he assured me that in most instances the "modernised touch" is traceable to the hectic and highly sensational films which are now being shewn so largely in India. Personally I am prepared to go a step further and assert that such experts in crime do not owe their tuition to the films but to some local "Oxford of Crime" or to imported criminals, whose sole occupation is to plan and direct. If we admit highly efficient criminal organisation in India, we must admit not only the influence but the personal direction of similar institution in London, Paris and New York.

CHAPTER XI.

THE PILGRIMAGE OF AZIR ALI.

I used to frequently visit a quarter of Calcutta infested with "kabob" shops. The culinary art predominated here and when Hatim Tai cried—"supper" all heeded him. At the extreme end of this thoroughfare was a "kabob" shop, yclept "The Mahommedan Restaurant" whose proprietor, Azir Ali, was an old friend of mine. Ali was a character. Destitute of all honour he gloried in the fact, but invariably swore by the Prophet that all "kabob" sellers, save only himself, were thieves and liars, and as he happened to be a "goonda" of a peculiarly ferocious type, none dared to contradict him. But Ali had a weakness—he was extremely superstitious and this was his undoing.

It all came about because Ali, who was undeniably the finest cook alive, attracted the major portion of the customers to his shop to the intense disgust and active animosity of the others—and then one day Ali received a letter. This he took from the postman very cautiously and looked at it long and ardently. At length he opened the envelope. Carefully he looked within. It contained nothing. In disgust he was about to throw it into the fire when something within arrested his attention. Ali drew it out carefully—it was a single hair and it was grey. He stroked his beard thoughtfully. What could this strange symbol portend? Then he started violently. The hairs in his own beard were grey!

The next day at precisely the same moment the postman handed Ali another letter. Another grey hair. Ali grew pale!

Again the next day at precisely the same moment the postman handed Ali still another letter.

One day Ali received a letter.

A single grey hair again. " By the beard of the Prophet" quoth Ali, "this is too much," and closed his shop early and went home.

That evening he consulted his favourite Mullah. "Are not the hairs on a man's head numbered?" remarked this dignatory when Ali had explained. "But" remonstrated Ali "these hairs are from some man's beard." The Mullah shook his head wisely. "Then they be all the fewer, my son" he remarked caustically.

Ali groaned.

Next morning early Ali returned to his shop. As he opened the door a little square patch of white attracted his attention. Carefully Ali examined the

"That evening he consulted his favourite Mulla."

mark. It was the mystic symbol of pisces. Now to the superstitious the sign of the fishes is at once lucky and unfortunate. It portends a voyage.

Maulvi Dil Muhammed sat in deep contemplation in the inner court of the Mosque of Akbar, which graces the head of Dhurrumtolla Street, when word was brought him that two devout Mussalmans desired to consult him. "Shew them in" said Dil Muhammed "and Allah grant their piety be not the offspring of penury." A moment later two evil-looking Mohammedans entered the Mosque and bowed reverently before the Mullah.

"Salaam Ali kum!" (The Peace of God be with you) Dil Muhammed greeted them effusively, for his sharp eyes had detected their avocations and remembering the visit of Azir Ali he anticipated much gain from this feud of the "kabob" sellers. "Be seated, friends—tell me your trouble. Mayhap I could advise you."

Thus greeted the rival "kabob" sellers poured out their grievances. Dil Muhammed listened patiently. "It is well" he said when they had concluded, "Azir Ali shall be dealt with. For the present hold thy peace and remember that those who give lavishly to the poor shall receive an hundredfold in Paradise."

The "kabob" sellers departed and Dil Muhammed secreting a couple of ten-rupee notes in the ample folds of his turban sat down to wait. And when the muizzem called the evening prayer and the lights had been lit in the sanctuary, Ali came hurrying through the gloom.

"Alas! alas!" he cried as soon as he had greeted the Mullah "much misfortune has come upon me. First it was the mysterious hairs and now I find the sign of the sacred fish upon my door." Dil Muhammed patted his friend's shoulder affectionately. "Calm thyself, Ali, and I will shew thee how thou mayest overcome thy enemies and gain great renown."

Next morning Azir Ali came late to his shop. Already was the hour for the morning meal much advanced and his numerous customers were growing impatient. When, however, his burly form was seen hastening down the street a sigh of satisfaction went up. Ali was a good cook and much appreciated in consequence. Hastening through the crowd, throwing back a cheery greeting to all, Ali thrust open his door and then started back with an exclamation of surprise—there upon the threshold! obvious to all, was the mystic symbol of the fishes! Friends and enemies alike crowded round to view the sacred sign. Ali waited for no comments from the spectators, but raising his voice began to praise God. "Surely am I the most blessed of all men" he cried "for see here on my threshold Allah hath placed the sacred sign of the twin fishes. 'Tis a symbol that I must journey far over the sea, and, look you, the fishes' heads point to the West. Need I remind you, brothers, that towards the West lies Mecca and the sacred tomb of the Prophet. Surely this is a sign from Heaven, a mark of special favour. Great honour is mine this day. Come, rejoice with me. Be my guests this morning. I am poor, yet will I feed all of you free, yea, even to the value of twenty rupees!"

Great was the cheering when Ali concluded and many congratulated him on his good fortune. At the Howrah Station that evening quite an admiring band of Ali's erstwhile guests assembled to wish him 'bon voyage.' Amongst them was Dil Muhammed, the Wise One, who, as he handed Ali his ticket, whispered—" Brother, 'tis only as far as Allahabad you need to travel. I have a cousin there who has an understanding mind. Stay with him the appointed time and when you return, forget not to stain thy beard a deep red."

Thus Azir Ali acquired great renown and fed

his friends at the expense of his enemies. But Dil Mohammed, the Wise One, smiled gravely, for had he not satisfied both parties?

This story helps to illustrate a point I wish to emphasize—the almost unbelievable credulity and superstition of the illiterate Indian. It is this weakness that makes him such an easy prey for imposters of all descriptions. It is, however, in the field of metaphysics and the supernatural that we find the most extraordinary examples of the extent to which these poor people can be led by unscrupulous agents. I quote from the "Statesman" of the 9th February 1929.

"Ashiq Ali, a hoary, eighty-year-old villager, who boasted the title of "Master of Ghosts," has just been given a forceful reminder that the cheating of credulous villagers has attendant dangers.

Ashiq traded on a reputation of being able to conjure up and control evil spirits, ghosts and *djinns* and to force them to reveal hidden treasure. Consequently he was gladly welcome into the home of a widow named Musammat Alam, who said she had so frequently dreamed that treasure was buried in her house that she had come to believe a search conducted by a fitting person would reveal real gold hidden somewhere under the floor of her house.

Her only fear was that there might be some difficulty in obtaining the treasure, for her visions had been made frightful by the sudden appearance of a hooded snake every time she stretched forth her hand to seize the jewels sparkling before her eyes.

Apparently Ashiq did not doubt his ability to unearth the treasure, but of course there were evil spirits not one, but a whole family of them, husband, wife and two children—who would have to be propitiated before they would think of yielding up their store of wealth. The only means of pleasing these spirits, Ashiq told the woman was by providing Rs. 15 to the "Master," who would see that the unseen beings were feted in a right royal manner.

The woman unhesitatingly parted with this sum of money and Ashiq went to his home.

Several days later Musammat Alam, the dreamer, sent Ali Bux, an *ekka* driver, to enquire whether the "Master" had succeeded in discovering where the treasure was hidden. Ali Bux found Ashiq in a great temper, for the latter had been tormented by the family of ghosts because the feast he had given them out of the woman's money was far from satisfactory. Another feast, he declared, was imperative if the treasure was to be found.

Again the widow parted with some of her money, but she informed the old "Master" that she could afford nothing further for the spirits.

Thereupon Ashiq came to the widow's house and went through an amazing ceremony. In one corner of her room he dug a small hole, which he covered with a cloth. Then he produced a bottle, placed it near the hole and went through a lengthy incantation. Suddenly he stood up and with a gesture of triumph displayed in the bottle a couple of small images in the shape of human children. These, he told the widow, were the ghost children, whom he had managed to capture with considerable difficulty. There yet remained the husband and wife, who were naturally much more obstinate and would require more money before they could be induced to come away from the wealth.

The widow was too impressed to think of resisting and she parted with the last of her savings.

Time, however, and the continued absence of Ashiq undeceived the widow who threatened to expose Ashiq to the police if he did not pay her back some of her money. Ashiq's courage was far from shaken. On the contrary, he next approached the *ekka* driver, Ali Bux, who had acted as the widow's emissary, and promised, for a consideration, to transfer the hidden wealth from the widow's house to that of Ali Bux. But the *ekka* driver had profitted by the woman's experiences and he was not prepared to part with any money until the "Master of Ghosts" gave him some tangible proof that the wealth was actually in his own house.

However, he invited old Ashiq to come to his house the following afternoon for any ceremony the latter might care to go through. Ashiq turned up at the appointed time and forthwith started his uncanny demonstrations. But instead of calling forth spirits he suddenly discovered to his extreme dismay that he had exorcised a live constable, who emerged from behind a curtain.

Ashiq saw that the game was up and he was more strongly convinced of this fact when Mr. S. W. Bobb, City Magistrate of Allahabad, sentenced him to four months' rigorous imprisonment on a charge of cheating.

CHAPTER XII

NIGHT HAUNTS OF CALCUTTA.

In spite of Police precautions, periodical raids and heavy sentences, the underworld of Calcutta, with its opium dens, its gambling hells and dancing girls, goes serenely on and it is to these haunts of iniquity I intend to introduce my readers so that, bereft and denuded of its glamour, they may have an opportunity of seeing the night haunts of Calcutta as they actually are.

Opium dens, particularly in the Chinese quarters of Calcutta, are much in vogue. There are two distinct classes of opium dens. There is the Opium Den proper, where the business of the evening is the actual smoking of opium, has-hish and other "dope." These are known only to a selected few and the system of entry is by personal introduction, passwords and signs. Fortunately for Calcutta, and thanks to a strict police vigilance, these Dens are few and far between. Of the other class of opium dens, which are in reality combined brothels, drinking saloons and gambling dens, I will have much to say later.

I can assure the reader that my first impression of an Opium Den proper was not a favourable one. My introduction and entry to this insalubrious spot was effected through an old Chinese Carpenter whom I had helped in various ways and who had for me a genuine regard.

"Ah Hing" I confided in him one day "I wish to see an Opium den. Will you take me?" He looked puzzled. "Opii, Opii" he muttered "no savee."

"You scoundrel" I said "you savee all right. Lead right on or I am done with you." The old celestial looked genuinely distressed. "Bad pase, bad pase" he admonished me. "You no savee. Him not nice man. He no likee you, why you come?"

I explained and at length after much alternate coaxing and threatening the old man gave way and a date was fixed. I waited in pleasurable anticipation, fully expecting to receive a summons from Ah Hing to sail out in the small hours of the morning to some secluded, evil smelling spot right in the heart of the slums. Imagine my surprise when one afternoon Ah Hing presented himself and announced his intention of taking me to an opium den right away.

"But Ah Hing" I remonstrated, "surely this is no time to visit an opium den?"

"Yah. You no savee" said the old man impatiently. "You come quick. I show you something" and I little knew what this something was he referred to. Following him to a waiting carriage we drove down a broad thoroughfare and pulled up at the door of a very respectable looking house. Here we alighted and entered a large Chinese Shoe Store. A young Chinaman came forward and politely enquired what we wanted, but I noticed a look of recognition pass between him and

Ah Hing, who drew him aside for a few minutes during which an animated conversation was held. That the young man was not too favourably impressed with me was evident from his looks and gestures, but the older man's arguments evidently prevailed, for after the conversation Ah Hing returned to me and bade me follow. I had noticed as I entered a small doorway, screened by a red curtain behind the counter. Through this door Ah Hing now led me into what appeared to be a long, badly-lit passage, which in turn led into a large low-roofed room, hung all round with heavy, but bright coloured curtains. Along the walls ran a broad dado of dark green on which were painted, in bright yellow, numerous geometrical figures, dragons and nude women running and leaping in the most impossible attitudes. We seated ourselves here and my attention was immediately arrested by a peculiar wizened-up creature whose skin, yellow and wrinkled with age, looked like parchment, seated before a small table at one end. This I discovered on enquiry was the "Master of Ceremonies" as it were. He it was who doled out the opium in previously filled slender bamboo pipes and took careful stock of all who came and went. Ah Hing politely enquired whether I would like a pipe and seemed rather disappointed when I refused somewhat hastily, but when I refused to let *him* smoke, I felt that the limit of his endurance had been reached.

"Where" I asked in order to distract his mind "is the special sight you were going to shew me."

At my question he brightened up considerably.

Scenes from the "Night Haunts" of Caicutta.

"Come" he whispered and rising led me towards another exit at the further end of the room. Reaching here we proceeded along a short passage till we came to a closed door before which an old Chinese woman sat. Ah Hing immediately accosted this old bedlamite and after a few whispered words, during which I saw a couple of rupees change hands, the old woman rose and going towards a little aperture in the wall unfastened a small window. Ah Hing bade me look and I did, but the sight I saw was one not calculated to impress me very favourably with opium dens and opium smokers—Ah Hing in particular. I am aware that the moral standards of East and West differ considerably and that the asceticism of the East must be viewed from a different stand point to that of the West, but Ah Hing's estimation of my moral qualities was certainly a painful shock to my own self esteem. On the carpeted floor of a room such as the one we had recently quitted were a number of girls, young maidens and old women, in various stages of somnolence and nudity. Those on whom the drug had already taken effect had been stripped of every vistage of clothing and laid so that they could be seen from the window through which I looked and it was to gaze and gloat over such a spectacle that Ah Hing had brought me. What I said to Ah Hing when we got out and what he thought are things that cannot be printed or explained.

If you take the Chitpore Car and travel to the extreme end of this road you will come to a quarter known as Sonagachi and to a lane bearing this name. This is a part of Calcutta to which decent people do not go and it is here the dancing girls are found.

Although it is a fairly accurate axiom that all Eastern dancing girls are prostitutes, yet it is scarcely correct to condemn all Eastern dances as vulgar. There are various styles of dances. Of these the hip-shaking variety predominate. The best known are the "Tandob", the "Lashab" or

"Pingal" and the "Deshi." The Tandob is really not a dance. There is nothing graceful about it, it is really a series of dancing exercises put to music. The "Deshi" is a country dance. Its figures and music are very similar to our early Barn Dances, but the "Lashab" or "Pingal" is certainly the most popular and graceful. It is impossible to describe the dance; it must be seen to be appreciated. Its principal characteristics are, however, quite distinctive. The dancer alternately places one hand on the hip holding the other above the head or works both before her in a snake-like attitude. She sways from the hip, keeping time to the music by shuffling her feet and jingling her "choories" (Bangles). This is the famous snake-dance of India and there is a tradition connected with the origin of this dance which is interesting. "Pingal" was the serpent who adorned the brow of "Mahadev" the great Rishi. One day when "Pingal" had left the protection of Mahadev to wander on the sea-shore, he was pounced upon by Gora (a snake eating bird) his mortal and hereditary enemy. In dire distress Pingal pleaded of "Gora" to spare his life offering to show him in return a wonderful dance, which would otherwise be lost to humanity. Gora agreed and at Pingal's request brought the "Apsras" (Heavenly dancing girls) to learn the dance. In order that the figures should not be forgotten, Pingal elected to dance in the sand so that the Apsras by following in his foot prints may learn quickly. Pingal then danced the famous snake dance, while the Apsras followed after him, and in reward was granted his life. This dance is consequently the most popular of all and no entertainment, in which dancing girls figure, is complete without it.

Sonagachi provides the visitor with a mixed bill of fare. If, in consideration of the locality, the moral tone or rather want of moral tone, he expects to witness scenes that are sensational, bizzare and unique, he is foredoomed to disappointment. Prostitution and its accompanying vices are seldom sensational, they are usually sordid and revolting, and in the badly-fit evil-smelling gullies and lanes of Sonagachi there is enough sordidness and evil to satisfy the most morbid minded. There are of course "Star class" performers among the dancing girls in this locality, and some of them have risen to a degree of local fame worthy of a better cause. Who has not heard of that beautiful, bewitching, dancing girl known as "Sonar-bai," through whose slender, henna-stained fingers, thousands of rupees slipped, easily earned and idly squandered. Her day was short, but while it lasted, glorious. At the tender age of ten, she was married to an aged, but wealthy zemindar, whom she left within a few years and took to the life of a dancing girl. Her beauty and skill soon attracted attention and Rajahs, zemindars and wealthy merchants courted her. Mistress of all, caring for none, Sonar-bai acquired untold wealth. It is said that in all she ruined seven Rajahs, ten zemindars and numerous wealthy merchants and ended herself, as all such careers of crime end, in destitution, abject poverty and want; despised by all, pitied by few and helped by none. But that there was some potential good in this woman is evident, for while she lived she lived lavishly, she fed the poor, gave to charity and in her closing years wrote a little pamphlet on her own life as a warning to those who seek the paths of evil.

I will now lead the reader to a different class of opium dens to those which I have mentioned before. These dens although outwardly simple places of amusement and restaurants of the poorer kind, are in actuality secret dens of iniquity. I remember well my first visit to one of these. It was situated in one of the less frequented parts of China town and was to all intents and purposes a Chinese eating house known as a "Chow Shop." "Chow" is a staple form of food for the Chinese of this quarter. It consists in finely sliced shreds of dough, cooked in lard and highly spiced. The flavour is peculiar and taste for this class of food is an acquired one. "Chow" in the hands of a professional Chinese cook, is certainly a most appetising and satisfying dish.

Entering the restaurant we were greeted by the proprietor himself, who at a whispered word or two from my companion led the way into a sort of back parlour or sanctum, where we were served with drinks (un-licensed) and "chow." After we had finished the tables were cleared and a number of Chinamen entered together with a fair number of guests of "other nationalities." The actual business of the evening now started. We crowded round the largest table and played various Chinese games of chance in which "Fan Tan" "Odd and Even" "Above and below Seven," all played with small shells (cowries) predominated. I took a hand in most of the games and lost in all about Rs. 30. My companion lost as well and I have no very distinct recollection of any one else winning except the proprietor, who was both host and banker.

When we had had enough of gambling, or in other words when we had all been cleaned out, the tables were removed, the guests retired to the various couches and chairs that lined the four walls and a fine Chinese mat was laid down in the centre of the room. A number of Chinese musicians now entered, bearing strange looking stringed instruments. On these they commenced to play at once and the melody they produced was of a quaintly beautiful, haunting type. After a few minutes there was a rustling of curtains and a young Jewish girl, as far as I could judge, entered. Although the melody was Chinese, this young performer executed quite a brilliant little performance in an entirely Eastern style and was followed by others equally graceful.

"So far so good," thought I. But I knew instinctively that it was not to regale us with such dances that these young performers had been brought. Gradually as the night wore on and as the liquor and opium cigarettes took effect, the character of the dances changed; growing gradually more and more lewd and repulsive, till just before I quitted the place: the scene was typical of the low, Eastern brothels, minus even the show of decency usually maintained in these places.

It is a peculiar characteristic of the white races that vice unveiled is repellant to most of us. It is probably due to a large admixture of puritan blood and that wonderful capacity we have for "taking our pleasures sadly."

CHAPTER XIII.

RELIGIOUS ASPECTS OF CRIME.

What the Cathedral is to the Christian, the ancient temple at Kalighat is to the Hindu. It is, in fact, the most celebrated place of pilgrimage in that vast district of Bengal known as the 24-Parganas.

The temple is situated on the bank of the old bed of the Ganges, two miles south of the southern boundary of Calcutta and owes its sanctity and situation alike to an ancient legend.

It appears that Daksha, the great Hindu Patriarch offered sacrifice to obtain a son but omitted to invite the God Siva. Sati, the daughter of Daksha, was married to Shiva and resented bitterly the insult thus offered to her husband. "Why" she demanded of her father "is my husband not invited? Why are no offerings made to him?" "Thy husband" was the reply "wears a necklace of skulls. How can he be invited to a sacrifice?" On hearing this Sati was so overcome with grief that she cursed her father and put an end to her own life. The bereaved husband thereupon took up her corpse and laying it on his shoulder started on a pilgrimage round the world, bemoaning his loss. Pitying his grief, and fearing destruction to the whole world, the gods ordered Vishnu, the Preserver, to relieve him of his burden.

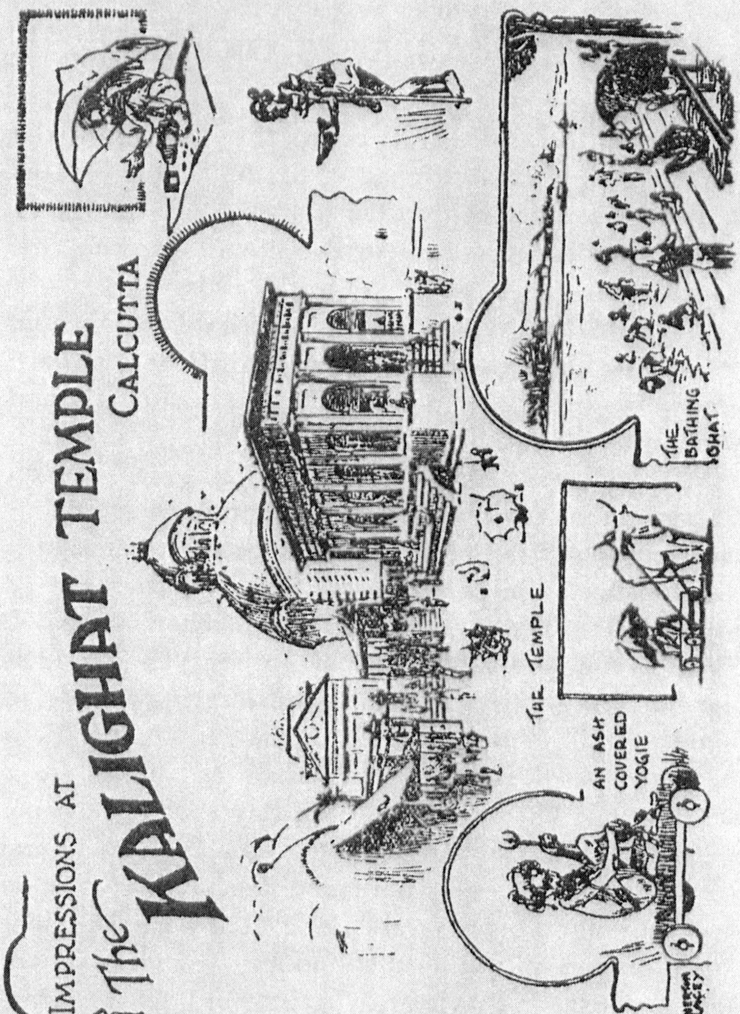
IMPRESSIONS AT
The KALIGHAT TEMPLE
CALCUTTA
THE TEMPLE
AN ASH COVERED YOGIE
THE BATHING GHAT

Vishnu immediately followed in the wake of Siva. and with his disc (sudarsan chakra) proceeded to back the corpse in pieces. Tradition has it that the body of Sati was divided in this way into 51 pieces and where each piece fell to the ground a temple was erected to her honour, so that there are in all 51 temples erected to Sati all over India. It was at Kalighat that one of her fingers fell and the Kalighat temple was accordingly erected on this spot. The temple itself is a very ancient structure. It is supposed to have been built three centuries ago by a member of the Sabarna Chaudhri family of Barisa who allotted 194 acres of land for its maintenance. A man named Chandibar was the first priest appointed to manage the affairs of the temple, and his descendants, who have taken the title of Haldar, are the present proprietors of the building. They have given up their priestly avocation and have amassed great wealth, not so much from the proceeds of the temple lands as from the daily offerings of the vast multitudes of pilgrims who flock to this shrine.

The temple itself is built in the typical Indian style. The present building, although retaining all its ancient features, has been considerably modernised. There is nothing particularly interesting in the building itself, the principal attraction to the visitor being in the various rites that are performed here during the Pujahs.

THE WORSHIP OF DURGA AND KALI.

The principal Hindu festival is the Durga Pujah. It is the worship of the Goddess Durga—

the manifestation of Divine power in female form. This Goddess is symbolised as a female having ten hands, and riding on a lion, and her worship assures for the devotee a life free from worries, ill-health and poverty.

Originally this festival was held during the month of Chaitra (March-April) for nine days, the whole period being called the Navaratri (nine nights). At present it is held in the moonlit half of the month of Aswin (September-October) and is the most celebrated festival of the year.

There is, of course, a legend connected with this change. It appears that King Ramachandra of Ayodhya, the hero of the Hindu epic "Ramayana" during his campaign against Ravana, the monster king of Ceylon prayed to the Goddess Durga for success. His prayers were heard and in the latter half of the month of Aswin, Ramachandra's armies were victorious. In thanksgiving, Ramachandra immediately ordered sacrificial offerings to be made to the Goddess Durga and the ceremony, so inaugurated, has continued to this day.

Hinduism is a personal religion. Although he may visit Kalighat during this festive season, the Hindu does it more as a pilgrimage to the shrine and to make votive offerings to the image of Kali. The pujahs themselves are performed at home, and the following is the usual system of celebration.

On the 15th July, (Rath Jathra) commonly known as the Car Festival the head of the house accompanied by the family *guru* or priest, selects a split piece of bamboo which he takes into the room in which his *penates dei* are kept. Here the bamboo is annointed with sandal-wood paste and prayers are offered to Vishnu and Durga. This bamboo remains here till September 3rd. (Janma Ashtami, the birthday of Krishna) when it is removed and employed in the construction of the idol. The mud used for this purpose is taken from the banks of the Ganges and when the image is complete is painted and adorned in the usual fashion. The main figure is that of Durga with ten hands bearing various weapons and is intended to symbolise her victory over Asura, 'the enemy of both gods and men. Around her are a number of lesser figures. These represent her two sons Karttikeya and Ganesa, Saraswati the wife of Brahma and Lakshmi the wife of Vishnu. There are also images of Mahesha, the buffalo-headed Asura whom Durga came to slay.

The initial ceremony is called the Bodhana or awakening of the Goddess. When the time arrives for the performances of this ceremony, the head of the family after certain purifications expresses his intention of performing the Puja. He then in due form appoints his *guru* as officiating priest, who in his name and on his behalf performs the various ceremonies. The ritual is long and tedious, the most interesting part of which is the invitation to the Goddess Durga to enter the house and dwell in the image prepared for her. During this part of the ceremony the priest lays his right hand on the breast of the image and recites the following incantation,

"Enter, O Divi, thou Mother divine,
"With thy eight Saktas. this home of mine.

"O Lotus Eyed one, respond to my prayers
"Protect me from sorrows, misfortunes and cares.
"Save me, Beloved, from dishonour, ill-health.
"Protect thou my children, my wives and my wealth.
"Enter, O Sankara, this image of thine,
"Fill its dead clay with thy spirit divine.
"Accept these small offerings, bless every gift.
"And from my poor shoulders all transgressions lift."

First the right eye, then the left, then the eye on the forehead are touched by the priest with an appropriate mantra, by which means the ceremony of "pranpratishta," or giving of life to the image, is performed. After this ceremony the various vessels and articles are blessed, and the image is now ready for worship.

On the conclusion of the Pujahs which usually last four days the Goddess is supposed to leave the image. To bid her farewell most elaborate ceremonies are gone through and on their conclusion the image is taken down from its platform. The women of the house then walk round it singing hymns and throwing rice-water and betel leaves upon it. It is then carried to the riverside or some convenient tank and there denued of all ornaments and valuables and then, amid the shouts of the spectators, cast into the water.

Where the pujah is conducted by a wealthy family or in large temples like Kalighat it is customary to offer sacrifices. Kids, goats and the like, up to the number of seven, are sacrificed, and

The famous Temple at Kalighat.

(By courtesy of the Publicity Officer, E. I. Ry.)

occasionally a buffalo is added. The victim is sanctified by the sprinkling of water from the sacred Ganges, and vermillion is placed on its forehead. The head is then made fast in a strong frame and, with one blow from the sacrificial knife, is severed. Portions of the flesh, with some of the blood is then placed before the image and dedicated to the Goddess.

Sacrifice is one of the essentials of Shiva worship. Kali is the wife of Shiva, the all-destroyer and all-producer. She is the most terrible of all deities in the Hindu pantheon. Her image is that of a female, her colour is black, her tongue protrudes several inches from her mouth. From the lobe of each ear a corpse is suspended and a string of human skulls ornaments her neck and breast. In each of her four hands is the head of a giant while prostrate below her feet lies the body of Shiva her husband.

In the hand of Sankara's followers and apostolic successors, Shiva-worship became one of the two chief religions of India. As at once the Destroyer and Reproducer, Shiva represented profound philosophical doctrines, and was early recognised as being in a special sense the god of the Brahmans. To them he was the symbol of death as merely a change of life. On the other hand, his terrible aspects preserved in his long list of names from the Roarer (Rudra) of the Veda to the Dread One (Bhima) of the modern Hindu Pantheon, well adapted him to the religion of fear and propitiation prevalent among the ruder non-Aryan races. Shiva, in his two-fold character, thus becomes the deity alike of the highest and of the lowest castes. He is the Mahadeva or the Great God of modern Hinduism; and his wife is Devi, pre-eminently the goddess. His universal symbol is the linga, a fetish emblem of reproduction, his sacred beast is the bull, connected with the same idea; a trident tops his temples. His images partake of his double nature. The Brahmanical conception is represented by his attitude as a fair-skinned man, seated in profound thought, the symbol of the fertilizing Ganges above his head, and the bull (emblem alike of procreation and of Aryan plough-tillage) near at hand. The wilder non-Aryan aspects of his character are signified by his necklace of skulls, his collar of twining serpents, his tiger-skin and his club with a human head at the end. His five faces and four arms have also their significance. His wife, in like manner, appears in her Aryan form as Uma, 'Light,' type of high born loveliness; in her composite character as Durga, a golden-coloured woman, beautiful but menacing, riding on a tiger; and in her terrible non-Aryan aspects, as Kali, a black fury, of a hideous countenance, dripping with blood, crowned with snakes and hung round with skulls. Shiva worship preserves in an even more striking way the traces of its double origin. The higher minds still adore the godhead by silent contemplation, as presented by Sankara, without the aid of external rites. The ordinary Brahman hangs a wreath of flowers about the phallic linga or places before it harmless offerings of rice. But the low-castes pour out the lives of countless victims at the feet of the terrible Kali, and until lately in the time of pestilence and famine, tried in their despair to appease the relentless goddess by human blood. During the famine of 1866, in a temple to Kali within 100 miles of Calcutta, a boy was found with his neck cut, the eyes staring open, and the stiff clotted tongue thurst out between the teeth. In another case at Hughli (a railway station only twenty-five miles from Calcutta) the head was left before the idol, decked with flowers. Such cases are true survivals of the regular system of human sacrifices which we have seen among the non-Aryan tribes. They have nothing to do with the old mystic purusha-Imedha or man-offering, whether real or symbolical, of the ancient Aryan faith, but form an essential part of the non-Aryan religion of terror, which demands that the greater the need, the greater shall be the propitiation. Such sacrifices are now forbidden, alike by Hindu custom and English law.

Immediately after the Pujas there takes place two Hindu Festivals of major importance. I refer to the "Kali Pujah" and the "Dewali" the local "Festival of Lights." The traditions connected with these pujas are so interesting and so typical of Hindu mythology that I describe them below, in detail:

The Kali Puja is an aftermath of the Durga Pujas and is devoted exclusively to the worship of "Kali" another manifestation of the Goddess Durga. It is held at midnight on the first day of the new moon which corresponds to the first day of the lunar month following the Pujas.

"Kali" as I have explained before is the dreaded Goddess of Destruction and, in her most familiar form, is represented as a dusky female standing astride the body of a male: she has a girdle of human hands, a necklace of skulls, her tongue protrudes from her mouth and her whole aspect is intended to inspire fear and dread.

This symbol of the Goddess owes its origin to a mythological source. It appears that the demons who inhabit the lesser worlds once grew so powerful that they attempted to storm the strong-hold of the Gods. In dire distress the Gods appealed to Shiva who to assist them created out of himself a ferocious female, whom he armed and sent amidst the demons to destroy them. This was Kali (or Sakthi) the Goddess of Destruction. Armed with the Kharga (sacrificial knife) Kali swept down on the demon hordes. With her second and lower left hand she grasped the King of the Demons by the hair, severing his neck with a single stroke. She proceeded to harass the demon forces till they fled and the Gods were saved. But Kali was now mad with the lust for blood and continued her victorious sway all over the world till the gods alarmed again at this awful slaughter, implored Shiva to recall her. But this was easier said than done. In vain Shiva implored her to return, his prayers were unheeded. At length he struck upon a bold ruse. Laying himself down among the slain, he placed himself directly in the path of the infuriated Goddess. In a moment Kali was upon him and feeling him stir beneath her feet bent down to destroy him. At that instant she recognized Shiva her progenitor, (and husband) and in her surprise remained transfixed over him. Realizing that she was nude, she cut off the hands of those she had slain and hung these as a girdle round her, and further to decorate herself, fashioned a garland out of the heads of her victims.

This mythological story accounts for the singular appearance of the Goddess. In the lower left hand she carried the head of the principal demon, in the upper the Kharga or sacrificial knife. Her upper right hand is raised as if bidding the Gods (righteous) have no fear and with her lower right hand she accepts the offerings of her devotees. Her protruding tongue symbolises her surprise on discovering the body of her husband among the slain.

The image is, of course, only an outward symbolism of a deeper esoteric meaning. In the worship of Kali the devotee praises the victory of good over evil, but it goes further, it illustrates how, in certain instances, even good, carried to excess, can result in evil.

The Puja itself is a very simple one. On the first day at midnight goats are offered and prayers said before the image to insure protection from evil. The next morning the image is carried in triumph through the city, and that same evening immersed in the sacred waters of the Ganges.

As this Puja synchronizes with the celebration of "Dewali" the two festivals are very often considered the same. This is incorrect. "Dewali" is really the birth of the cold weather and as this night is supposed to be the darkest in the year, choraghs (oil lamps) are burnt, crackers fired to drive away the powers of darkness and fire balloons sent up to supplement the natural illumination of the sky. It is also a period of rejoicing and feasting.

I will now turn to the influence such beliefs have on the minds of the more ignorant part of our rural population.

Human sacrifice is by no means extinct in India. It is still indulged in to an extent seldom realized by the average man. I have witnessed myself, not the actual sacrifice, but the ghastly remains, and in confirmation of the above statement will quote from recent Press Reports.

AUTHENTIC INSTANCES OF HUMAN SACRIFICE.

That this awful practice has not yet ceased in India, the two following authentic cases will shew. I have selected these two instances from recent Press Communiques. The first case is reported from Jubbulpore on March 22nd 1925, and runs as follows:—

"A sensational trial before Mr. A. D. Barr, Sessions Judge, and four assessors, at Mandla, has just terminated.

According to the evidence, one, Mulchand, who was in the Government service and has since been engaged as a petition writer at Mandla, lived there with his family consisting of three sons, namely, Chotey Singh, Bhopat Singh, Luchman Singh, a daughter, Rukhman, and a daughter-in-law Janki, wife of Bhopat Singh.

Luchman Singh was a boy of 14 years of age and on or about December 15, 1924, he fell ill. Medical treatment proving ineffective, the family believed that the boy was "possessed," and that, in order to obtain his recovery, a human sacrifice was necessary.

The woman Janki, it was stated, first severed the tip of the girl, Rukman's little finger, and put some of the blood on a piece of bread which was taken to a place where a certain holy man usually sat. Finally the girl was killed as a sacrifice to the goddess Kali.

This proving ineffective the patient, Luchman Singh was starved, and despite the bitter cold he was taken, bound hand and foot, naked, and, deposited in the open near where the holy man sat. It was hoped this treatment would serve to drive out the "devil" but it actually caused the boy's death.

The other members of the family were arrested and tried on a charge of murder before four assessors who found them not guilty on the ground that though Luchman Singh died from cold and exposure, it was not intended to cause his death. As regards the killing of the girl Rukman, the accessors held that the guilt of the accused was excused because they all believed that, by this human sacrifice, they were but obeying the dictates of a divine being.

The Sessions Judge said he was inclined to agree with the assessors that the accused, in their treatment of the boy Luchman Singh, did not intend to cause his death. But as regards the girl Rukman, he was clearly of opinion that she was murdered as a sacrifice to Kali. The Sessions Judge said he must reject the assessors' view on this point as it would be to encourage such murders. He therefore sentenced the woman Janki to transportation for life, and the remaining accused, Mulchand, Chotey Singh and Bhopat Singh to death subject to confirmation by the Judicial Commissioner, Nagpur."

The next case is from Kishoreganj and was reported briefly on May 18, 1925.

"A report has reached here from a village three miles from the town that a twelve-year old Namasudra boy was sacrificed before the goddess Kali on the last Ambasya day. The dead body of the boy with some flower and betel leaves, was found on the next morning under a tree."

This question of human sacrifice leads me naturally to the question of suicides. Yellow arsenic, aconite, opium and copper sulphate seem to find favour with both sexes, but the method, par excellence, for young girls who find themselves unhappy in their married or home live, is to soak their garments with kerosine oil and burn themselves to death, usually on the house-tops. This extra-ordinary and painful method of committing suicide I am inclined to attribute to the profound and lasting effect the practice of "Suttee" must have had on the minds of Hindu women scarcely a generation ago. If the reader will remember that as recently as 1823, the official records shew as many as 575 cases of "Suttee," the moral and physiological effect of this barbarous social custom on the minds of Hindu girls will be better understood. The practice of "Suttee" is so unusual that I feel sure a short account of this extraordinary social custom will be found deeply interesting.

A HISTORICAL ACCOUNT OF "SUTTEE" OR WIDOW BURNING.

When the British Government in India stamped out the practice of Suttee (self-immolation of widows) there was abolished one of the most amazing ceremonies that have been known in any country in the world. Over 100 years ago Lord William Bentinck instituted an Act which made Suttee unlawful, and since then, under the influence of Western civilisation, the country has forgotten that once upon a time not less than two widows were burnt upon their husbands' funeral pyres every day of the year. What an appalling waste of human life! That is the exclamation which immediately springs to one's lips on learning that fact—every year at least 700 women sacrificed. But still greater is the sense of wonder when one remembers that "Suttee" was known and practised in India, more than 3,000 years ago.

Diodorus Siculus, in his narrative of the Expedition of Alexander the Great into India, tells us that Suttee originated from the crime of a woman who destroyed her husband by poisoning him. He describes a contest which took place between the two wives of the leader of the Indian troops, Ceteus, for the privilege of burning on the funeral pile of their husband. The contest was decided in favour of the younger wife, and, Siculus continues: "She who had lost her cause departed weeping, rending the veil which had covered her head, and tearing her hair, as if some great calamity had been communicated to her. The other, rejoicing at her success, proceeded to the funeral pile, crowned by the females of her household with mitres. She was decked with ornaments as if for a nuptial festival and was attended by her relations, chanting a song in praise of her virtue. At length, having embraced her family, she was placed upon the pile by her brother and to the great astonishment of the people who had assembled to witness the ceremony, she terminated thus heroically her life. The widow, bending towards her husband's body, uttered no pusillanimous cry when the flames began to roar, which excited towards her the pity of some of the spectators, whilst others exrolled her."

The length of this quotation from an ancient writer is justified by the valuable information it provides; it gives us facts which should be borne in mind when considering the difficult problem which confronted the British when, centuries later, they sought to eradicate the custom from the country. Suttee was extolled by all; the widow who sacrificed herself in the flames of her husband's pyre was revered by her relatives; she was assisted in every way in the performance of that ordeal; kings not only lent their countenance to the practice, but expected that their widows would go with them through the shades of death. All these facts, receiving added honour from centuries of tradition, made the institution in time almost ineradicable.

Wonder is naturally aroused by the knowledge that a family would assist one of its members to perform Suttee. That sentiment, however, is dispelled when it is known that relationship with a Suttee gave a certain rank in India. Thus the son of a woman who had sacrificed herself in this manner was ranked above his fellows who could not boast the same distinction; if his sister had also burnt herself, he was ranked proportionately higher in popular esteem; and if still others of his family had sacrificed themselves, he was invested with the dignity of a king. Little wonder the male members of a family encouraged rather than prevented the self-immolation of their womenfolk.

Then, too, the widow herself achieved immortal fame. Suttee, in Sanscrit, means "a good wife," and when a widow was described as having performed Suttee, it meant that she had become a model partner: no higher praise could be conferred upon any Indian woman.

From the year 1815 attempts were made to record all cases of Suttee which took place in India and we have the following "returns" for six divisions, or commissionerships in Bengal:—In 1815 the widows who burned themselves numbered 378; in 1816 there were 442; in 1817, 707; in 1818 650; in 1820, 597; in 1821, 654; in 1822, 513; and in 1823, 575—making a gross total in nine years of 5,425 individuals who had thus perished, and that only in a portion of Bengal, be it remembered. Taking into account those who must also have been burnt in the Madras and Bombay Presidencies, the total number would be well over 6,000. In short, two women on an average calculation were destroyed in that manner in India on every day of the year.

Students who have delved into the subject aver that a Suttee, before she sacrificed herself, fortified herself with drugs which practically deprived her of her senses. But this matters little even if correct; the fact remains that the curious practice was generally voluntary.

Two authentic instances of Suttee, among the last to be performed in India, are on record. Mrs. Fanny Parks described the following case as having been performed in Allahabad in 1822: "A corn chandler having died, his widow declared her intention of being burnt with him, though the Magistrate offered her a considerable sum of money to relinquish her design. In reply she threatened to hang herself in the magistrate's kutcherry, if he attempted to interfere with her, affecting to believe that she had been burnt six times with her husband, and that the forthcoming would be the seventh time of cremation. As no food or water may be taken between the death of a husband and the self-sacrifice of his widow, the magistrate deferred the ceremony for two days; but all in vain. The pile was therefore built up; the body duly placed, and guards stationed to keep back the crowd, which was estimated at 5,000 people. The widow, clad in a red robe, bathed in the Ganges and with a burning brand in her head, walked, with a cheerful countenance, round the pyre, applied the torch, and calmly ascended. Laying her husband's head upon her lap, she rapidly repeated a formula, until the wind blew the flames upon her, when she sprang to her feet, and approached the side as if to jump off. A man with raised sword drove her back, and was instantly arrested by the magistrate. The widow then leapt down and ran to the river, her arms and legs alone being slightly scorched. Having slaked her thirst, she now offered to mount the pile a second time, but the magistrate laid his hand upon her shoulder; and by his touch rendered her impure. Her religion of itself forbade a second attempt."

The second instance was described in the course of a long debate in the India House on the 28th March, 1827, on a resolution, moved by a Mr. Poynder, regarding the burning of Indian widows:—

One Seethoo died when absent from his family. A fortnight afterwards, his widow, Hoomulea, a girl of about 14 years of age, proceeded to burn herself, the pile being prepared by her nearest relation. The preparatory rites completed, Hoomulea ascended the pile, which was fired by her uncle, Sheolal. The agony was soon beyond endurance, and she leapt from the flames; but, seized by Sheolal and others, she was taken up by the hands and feet and again thrown upon it. Much burnt, and her clothes quite consumed, she again sprang from the pile, and running to a well hard by, laid herself down in the watercourse, weeping bitterly. Disregarding her entreaties, however, Sheolal seized her again and cast her on to the flames, which immediately consumed her.

In future ages, while there is yet a memory or a record of the ceremony of Sutee, one particular story will always be mentioned. This story concerns the incomparable Job Charnock, the founder of Calcutta. Job, we gather from the diary of William Hedges, went one day to see a young widow burn herself on her husband's funeral pyre; but "he was so smitten with the widow's beauty that he sent his guards to take her by force from her executioners, and conduct her to his lodging." Charnock apparently married the widow and the couple had several children. They settled in Calcutta, and after many years their loving attachment was severed by the death of the woman. He kept the anniversary day of her death by sacrificing a cock.

THE PRACTICE OF SELF IMMOLATION.

I now come to the last and final phase of this revolting practice of human sacrifice. The fanatic Hindu, finding that all other means to propitiate the gods have failed, very often offers himself up as a holocaust, hoping thereby to appease the angry gods who ravage his humble home every year with plagues and famines and pestilences and so save at least his wives and children. This "sacrifice" takes many forms, few of which ever terminate in the death of the "victim." But the sufferings endured are real, and the earnestness and devotion displayed are pathetic.

I recount a case of "self-immolation" which I recently saw. Early in February 1926, I visited a small station on the Bengal Nagpur Railway called Santalahi, situated in the heart of the coal mining districts, where I witnessed the wonderful "Hook-swinging" Ceremony. For the benefit of those who have never seen this curious custom I will describe the ceremony in detail. Towards the close of the Mela which precedes this ceremony, priests call for volunteers and appear to have no difficulty in finding many. The "victims" are stripped to the waist, garlanded with flowers and made to sit in rows. One of the priests now advances. With one hand he grasps firmly the fleshy part of his victim's back just below the shoulder blade. Pulling firmly on the skin he appears to separate the epidermis from the flesh. With one quick thrust he then forces a sharp pointed hook, of the same variety as those on which meat are hung, through the skin. When both shoulders have been treated in this fashion, the victim is led with much singing and shouting and beating of tom-toms, to a bamboo platform raised some twenty feet off the ground. Here ropes are inserted into the free ends of these hooks and attached to a stout pole, the free end of which is made fast to a rotating beam embedded firmly in the soil below this platform. The victim is now garlanded afresh. Bells are tied to his feet and when all is ready he is swung off this platform, hanging only by these hooks, and rotated slowly round and round. During this process the victim chants hymns, distributes flowers and supplicates divine favours. This swinging seldom lasts more than five minutes, after which the victim is released, the hooks abstracted and the flesh firmly pressed so that the punctures are practically closed. This ceremony is possibly a modernised survival of the old "Merish" or human sacrifice. The gods of the ignorant villager are best appeased with blood.

Human blood was pre-eminently the most acceptable and during times of famine, pestilence and flood, human lives were freely offered that the gods might be satisfied. The swinging of a human body, suspended only with flesh hooks, to all points of the compass, is therefore symbolical and to the ignorant mind possibly serves the purposes as well.

CHAPTER XIV

THE GANGA SAGAR MELA AND CHILD SACRIFICE.

Annually about the 15th January there is a great exodus of pilgrims from Calcutta. These people flock into the city from all parts of the country and are shipped down the Hooghly in the B. I. S. N. Co's steamers. This is known as the Ganga Sagar Mela and something about the history of this island and the festival held here will prove interesting.

The island itself lies at the mouth of the Hooghly River. The northern extremity of the island, which is about 25 miles long, is called "Mud Point" and is the site of the telegraphic station. At its south-western angle stands the old Sagar Lighthouse, originally built in 1808.

The reclamation of the island was started in 1811 by a Mr. Beaumont, who received a grant of 100 acres of land from the Government of Bengal to start a leather industry. Mr. Beaumont appears to have abandoned this scheme and later applied for a further grant of land on a cultivating tenure. This was refused, but in 1820 the Government appears to have sanctioned the lease of the entire island to an association composed of European and Indians on a nomial rental for the purpose of cultivation. The project was begun with vigour but dropped within the year when it was discovered that as the jungle lands were cleared the sea encroached further on the island, the sandy beach not having sufficient tenacity to resist its invasion.

In 1819, Mr. Trower, Collector of the 24-Perganas, originated a company called the Sagar Island Society and made another determined effort to reclaim and develop part of this island. His efforts were attended with partial success and the centre of the island was named after him, Trowerland. In the cyclone of 1833, however, the entire work was destroyed and the project again abandoned. Four Europeans appear to have next taken over part of the northern island and to have started the maufacture of salt and the cultivation of rice. But this also was destroyed in the cyclone of 1864 when 4,137 persons, or about three-fourths of the entire population of the island perished. Of later years portions of the northern island have come under cultivation, but the south is still under dense jungle.

The Ganga Sagar Mela is held annually about the middle of January at the time known as Makara Sankranti, (1st Magh) when the sun enters the zodiacal sign of Capricorn, and during this period thousands of pilgrims flock to the island to bathe in the sacred waters of the Ganges. There is an interesting legend in conection with this bathing festival which accounts for the great sanctity of this spot.

Sagar, King of Oudh, the thirteenth ancestor of Rama, had performed the Aswamedha jajna, or horse-sacrifice, ninety-nine times. This ceremony consisted in sending a horse round the earth with a challenge to all to arrest its progress. If the horse returned unopposed, it was understood to be an acquiescence in the supremacy of the challenger and the animal was then solemnly sacrificed to the gods. When King Sagar made preparations for the hundredth sacrifice, Indra, King of Heaven, who had himself performed the ceremony a hundred times grew jealous and stole the horse, concealing it in a subterranean cell where the sage Kapila, or Kapilmuni was absorbed in meditation, dead to all external occurrences. The sixty-thousand sons of Sagar traced the horse to its hiding place and believing the sage to be author of the theft assaulted him. The holy man thereupon cursed them and they were burnt to ashes and their souls cast into hell. A grandson of Sagar, hearing of the occurrence, came to Kapilmuni and begged him to redeem the souls of the dead, but the sage replied that if the waters of Ganga could be brought to the spot, then only could this be accomplished.

Ganga was at this time residing in Heaven in the custody of Brahma the Creator. The grandson of Sagar prayed to him to send the goddess to earth but died before his supplications were heard. Bhagirath his son miraculously born to his widow after his death then took up his supplications and Brahma permitted Ganga to visit the earth. Bhagirath led the way as far as Hathiagarh, in the 24-Perganas, near the sea, and then declared that he could not show her the rest of the way. Ganga, thereupon, in order to make sure of reaching the spot, divided herself into a hundred mouths, thus forming the delta of the Ganges. One of these mouths reached the cell of the sage and by washing away the ashes completed the atonement and the souls of the sons of Sagar were released from hell. Ganga thus became the sacred stream of a hundred mouths, and at its junction with the sea at Saugar Island is found the most celebrated place of pilgrimage in Bengal.

The religious part of the festival usually lasts only three days. The ceremony opens with a propitiation of the ocean. This consists in casting various offerings into the water with short ejaculatory prayers. The oblations are commonly fruits and flowers, but a favourite offering among the richer pilgrims is known as the "panch ratna" or five gems. This consists in a pearl or diamond, an emerald, a topaz, a piece of coral, a coconut, an areca-nut and the sacred thread worn by the Brahmans.

There is a temple here dedicated to Kapilmuni. The image is a shapeless block of stone daubed with red paint. In front of the temple is a banyan tree under which are images of Rama and Hanuman. Offerings are usually made by suspending a piece of earth or brick to a bough of this tree with a short prayer of solicitation. Behind the temple is a shallow pool called Sitakund. This is filled with fresh water, probably from some underground reservoir. Here the pilgrim is permitted to sip a small quantity of the sacred water on payment of a fee to the manager of the temple, and is led to believe that the water never decreases as it is fed from a miraculous source.

Formerly this festival, like a great many early religious rites of this character, was made an occasion for offering human sacrifice. The sea around Saugar Island and its numerous waterways, teem with crocodiles and many a Hindu mother has thrown her first born to these awful creatures in the devout belief that her sacrifice will prove acceptable and provide a *via media* for many future offspring.

The practice of infanticide is by no means uncommon in India. It is resorted to as a means of getting rid of inconvenient offspring, especially female children, whose advent in poor families, already overburdened in this respect, amount to nothing short of a calamity, but it is in its religious aspect that infanticide presents some extraordinary features. Barren women frequently resort to child murder in the hope of securing children of their own. Instances are on record where the murdress bathed her own body in the still warm blood of her innocent victim buoyed up by the hope that so potent a method must of necessity result in the re-birth of the dead child in her own womb, a method strangely reminiscent of the notorious Gilles de Retz in fifteenth-century France.

But it is not only for the purpose of securing offspring that this practice is resorted to. Children are frequently sacrificed to appease the wrath of some deity or to obtain divine favours. We have all read sensational accounts where children have been buried alive in the foundations or main walls of some important building to ensure the success of the scheme. But sometimes the sacrifice takes a novel turn and the child is offered up to appease an evil spirit whose resting place has been disturbed or hidden treasure removed. I quote a typical instance from a recent Press Report. The story comes to us from Secunderabad and is dated the 28th November 1926.

"The story of a remarkably gruesome crime, alleged to have been committed by a rich woman about three years ago in order to appease evil spirits supposed to be the guardians of a treasure trove is contained in the Hyderabad State Police report for 1333 fasli.

One Radhama, Patwarni or Yelamner, in the Nalgonda District, asked a Kunbi woman to procure for her a first born infant girl for the purpose of unearthing a treasure trove buried in her house and promised the Kunbi a reward for her services. The Kunbi woman waited for an opportunity and, seeing the 18-month old daughter of a local goldsmith playing in the street, kidnapped the child and took it to Radhama, who hid it in the upper storey of her house, giving it a strong dose of opium to keep it quiet. At nightfall Radhama went to the spot where the treasure trove was supposed to have been buried, accompanied by four men. Then, while one of the men chanted incantations, the other men excavated the ground.

The report goes on to say that when the treasure trove had been found the baby girl was fetched from the place where it was concealed and brutally sacrified to the guardian spirits and buried in the pit from which the treasure was removed. The woman and her accomplices obtained bail but on revision the Sessions Court annulled the bail order. The woman then moved the High Court and secured an order for her release on bail. The Full Bench, however, ordered the woman to be kept under special surveillance and the police investigation to be continued. Subsequently H. E. H. the Nizam appointed a commission to enquire into the case. The findings of this commission are not known."

This brings me to a very interesting phase of this system of sacrifice. It is known locally as "Head Cutting Scares." Recent riots and communial tension in Calcutta demonstrated how real were the beliefs in this myth and how liable to stir up panic and cause blood-shed. "Head Cutting" has its origin in a very ancient source. I am not prepared to vouch for the authenticity of such "legends," but it is fairly universally believed that during the early days of the Mogul invasion before a building, edifice or structure of any importance could be erected, the local satrap would send out his troops with orders to secure a certain number of children for sacrificial purposes in order to ensure the success of the scheme.

This tradition has lived in the minds of the more ignorant part of the population and when it is remembered that our coolies, masons, blacksmiths and in fact all classes of menial labour, are drawn mainly from this source; the horror, the universal panic caused amongst these people when it is rumoured that the Government has sent out spies to entrap children for sacrifice, can readily be understood. Calcutta has suffered a good deal from panics of this type, but that "Head Hunting Scares" are not confined to cities alone, the following account, kindly furnished by an old Planter of my acquaintance, will show.

HEAD HUNTING SCARES IN THE TEA DISTRICTS.

It was while I was employed as a Manager of one of the Tea Estates in the Dooars that the events I am about to narrate befell. In my daily rounds on horseback through the estates, my evening inspection of the day's collecting, I became acutely conscious of a feeling of pent-up emotion, restrained excitement and even active animosity, among the garden coolies of both sexes. Anyone acquainted with the management of tea gardens in India, will understand my anxiety. The labourers in our gardens are usually a care-free, jolly lot, seldom resentful of punishment and never vindictive. Their present attitude was, therefore, all the more incomprehensible. In vain I questioned the Sardar. "Was the rice of a very poor quality?" "No huzur." "Was there any sickness in the lines?" "No huzur?" "Then why were the men dissatisfied?" He could give no explanation, but I was aware, all the time, that he was hiding something from me. The more I questioned him the more mysterious he became contenting himself by saying "Bhout kharab bat" "Bhout kharab bat" (Very bad news, very bad news) and that was about all that I could get out of him.

The next phase of this extraordinary situation was more perplexing still.

I first noticed that the village parawallah had disappeared. This is a grave symptom and usually heralds a local dacoity. However as time went on and no dacoity occurred I made enquiries and ascertained that the man had just simply vamoosed. A few mornings later I received another shock, the local postman deposited the total correspondence of the entire village on my front verandah, refusing absolutely to go to the coolie lines to deliver the mail. And then, before I could make any further move in the matter, came black tragedy.

I was out one morning superintending the plucking. Suddenly from a distant part of the garden, came a sound of women wailing. In a moment every coolie had dropped his basket and rushed towards the spot. In some trepidation I galloped through the crowd, forcing my way right up to the spot where three or four coolie women sat on the ground, wringing their hands and crying after the fashion of Indian women, whose nearest and dearest are dead.

"What is the matter" I shouted angrily.

"Her child has been stolen, huzur" some of the men nearest me answered.

"Stolen? Rubbish," I cried "who would steal a child?"

There was an ominous silence.

Then once again the wailing started. "See, here is where I laid him, brothers," she moaned. "Here are his swathling clothes. Here besides this bush he lay—so playful and sweet. And then came the evil one and stole him. Oh, my son, my son, never shall I see him again" and so, on and on, while I realized that another ten minutes of this and the men would be completely out of hand. I determined to organize a search party immediately. Something had to be done and done quickly and with this intention I turned to address the men, when I was interrupted by fresh shouting from an entirely different quarter. With one accord the men turned and rushed towards the sound and I was left alone with the wailing women nor was I left long in doubt as to the turn of affairs things had taken. There was a sudden cry of "Maro, Maro" (Kill, Kill) followed by a blood-curdling shriek, as of some being in mortal agony and then silence. Once again I forced my way through the crowd and then all but fainted at the ghastly sight before me. On the ground lay an old man, his

I lifted one end of the bag, spilling the contents

face and skull battered to a pulp and his body lacerated with knife thrusts.

"Who has done this?" I stammered. There was no reply. Then a voice from the midst of the crowd shouted, "It is he who stole the child." Immediately there was a chorus of affirmations. The wildest statements were made. The victim had not only stolen the child that morning but hundreds of others besides; and there in his bag were the heads of poor innocents he had decoyed and sacrificed. I waited till the babble had subsided and then lifted the bag lying besides the corpse, at one end spilling the contents on the group—it consisted of a few green cocoanuts. In the silence that followed I found my tongue. Every curse, every vituperative, every expletive I could remember or conjure up I heaped on their heads. Those were the days of hard swearing and I was reckoned something of an adept in this line, but I felt that morning I had reached the zenith of my abilities—it was a perfect panegyric of vituperation, of hate and loathing. Nor did I pause for breath till I discovered that my only audience was the poor, mangled remains of the old man lying at my feet.

There was the usual police enquiry, of course, and next day in company with the District Magistrate I summoned the Sardar to the bungalow. He appeared smiling, but looked slightly uncomfortable when he observed the Magistrate.

"Well," I interrogated him, "what have you to say for yourself and yesterday's doings?"

At my question he looked surprised.

" Yesterday " he said addressing the Magistrate direct, " I was at the Sahib's bungalow clearing his top-boots, saddles and guns. When the Sahib returned I took his horse to the stables, watered and fed him and then went home. The Sahib knows I am telling you the truth."

I nearly collapsed. This was the rascal who had practically led the excited coolies the day previous and here was he calmly citing me as principal witness in his defence. I was about to make an appropriate retort when a wink from the District Magistrate silenced me.

The Magistrate was an adept at obtaining information.

"Of course, Sardar," he replied, "we know you were not there. But tell me, the coolies on this garden are great fools."

The Sardar spat disdainfully. " Great fools, Sahib, great fools."

" And they talk much that is stupid "

" It is to be expected, Protector of the Poor."

" What did they say about this man who was murdered ? "

The Sardar looked uncomfortable. " They said he was a spy, huzoor, in the pay of the Sarkar.'

" A spy ? But it was well known that he was only a vendor of cocoanuts."

" That may be, Sahib, but as I said before, these coolies are great fools and probably thought otherwise."

" But what else would he sell, besides cocoanuts ? "

The Sardas was silent for fully a minute, before he spoke. "May be heads—childrens' heads, huzoor? The Sarkar pays a high price for these things."

Both the Magistrate and I remained silent.

For a while the Sardar looked uncomfortable. He shuffled his feet and settled his turban and at last unable to contain himself burst out with all the information we knew was seething within him. It was a long tale, but it told us what we wanted to know. It appears that the Public Works Department were erecting a new iron bridge over the Jaldacca and were sinking concrete piles for supporting the main girders. The success of this scheme was a matter of much speculation among the local natives who were well aware of the unstable nature of the river bed and the sandy soil. It was just this uncertainty that was the mainspring of the trouble. How it started no one knew, but it was soon rumoured that the success of the bridge depended on the propitiation of the local river gods and spirits and as usual only human sacrifice could accomplish this. Children were the sacrifice, par excellence and their heads were required for throwing into the pits dug for the concrete piles, to scare away the evil spirits. The cocoanut vendor's inopportune arrival with his bag and its suggestive contents, just as a child was thought missing, was fatal at the moment, and the storm burst.

This was the cause of the tension in the coolie lines and the story the Sardar told, explained it, but there was more to follow.

His account to the District Magistrate satisfactorily concluded, the Sardar turned to me with a bright smile.

"Sonia has found her baby, Sahib. It was sleeping under the next bush,"—then again his face clouded, "but the Sahib was very angry and said many evil things concerning us and our fathers and mothers . . . . . ."

"Yes," I retorted, "and I would like to say some more." The Sardar looked alarmed.

"But why, huzoor? 'Tis a pity we killed him, but the man was old and would have died sooner or later."

And that was all.

CHAPTER XV

TALE OF THE SAKCHILLI.

The Sakchilli* sat on the fence that bordered the Raja's poultry-yard and gazed wistfully at the royal chickens. His raiment was of the simplest. A piece of string, encircling his waist, upheld a four-inch piece of rag—the only garment he possessed. For the rest he went as Nature had clad him.

But the Sakchilli was not content. Although his garments were breezy, his stomach was empty, and he was filled with a great longing as he gazed at the Raja's fat chickens.

"Surely," he thought, "my Master, the Raja, is generous. He will not miss a chicken or two and there is always my brother the jackal to blame. But who is this that comes in such a hurry? Surely it is Sonia, the ill-begotten offspring of that aged screech-owl,—the Metarani. So! she comes to feed the geese,—birds of a feather truly! Ho! there, stupid! Would you choke that bird with food? Cramming so large a piece down its gullet! Alas! I insult these birds when I class you with them." But the inopportune arrival of the Syce put a stop to this soliloquy.

"Be off, villain!" he shouted "before I bring my

---

*A madman—more knave than fool.

whip." The Sakchilli waited to hear no more. Already he was hastening down the great, white road that led to the City. And as he hurried along he observed with surprise a great concourse of people proceeding in the same direction.

"Brothers," he accosted them, "why do you hurry to the City to-day? Is there a 'hat,' or does our gracious master, the Raja, hold a durbar?" But no one would answer him, while some cried "Hutto, pagla!" (move out, madam) and hurried on faster.

Now the Sakchilli was genuinely amazed. "What could it be" he thought, "that makes these

"Here," he cried, "is the thief."

fools hurry so?" and then he remembered his friend the leper who sat at the city gates.

"Tell me, O! Rotten One," he cried, as he reached the leper's side, breathless with running, "why do all these fools hasten to the city?"

The leper favoured him with a withering glance. "My friend," he replied, "your brain rots quicker than my body, and if your ears be not stopped with the filth you eat, listen and I will tell you. It is reported that the King's most precious diamond has been stolen and even now a Royal Proclamation is being made, offering a mighty reward to the one who restores that gem. Money, Mad One, attracts fools like the sweets sold by yonder rogue attract the flies. So hasten now. Mayhap you may succeed, for of all the fools that hurry by, surely thou art the greatest."

* * * * *

"Listen listen! people of Delhi! Our gracious master, the Raja, offers one lakh of rupees to the man who restores his diamond and an honoured position in his household. Let him who has knowledge speak. Let the robber restore. There will be no punishment for either!"

Scarcely had the town crier ceased when the Sakchilli cried out—"I have the diamond, give me the reward!" And a moment later regretted he had ever been so foolish as to say such a thing. For those nearest, fell upon him crying "Thief! thief!" while others anxious to secure the reward grasped him by the limbs, pulling him this way and that, crying—"Let go, I seized him first. He is mine" and in a moment the Sakchilli would have been torn to pieces, had not the Raja's soldiers, fearing a riot, hurried to the scene and rescued him.

It was a very sore and very repentant Sakchilli that knelt in the presence of his Royal Master a few minutes later.

"Well, Madmam! Where is the diamond?"

"Diamond? What diamond?" The Sakchilli looked amazed.

The Raja motioned to his Syce. "Bring me that whip," he said, "perhaps that will restore his memory." But the Sakchilli's memory was already perfect,—he had seen the Syce.

"Protector of the Poor!" he wailed, "give me time. This gem has been very cleverly hidden and

Flung him in the tank

I must search for it" and then he remembered his greatest longing, that he should sit and witness a durbar like a Raja himself.

"Bring forth all the Royal elephants," he demanded.

The Raja and his whole court sprang up in amazement. "Royal Elephants!" "What for?" "Lunatic!" "Throw him out!" In vain they reasoned and argued—the Sakchilli was determined. It was going to be the Royal Elephants or nothing. So with a groan the Raja gave way and after a while the State Elephants, gaily bedecked and caparisoned, passed in solemn procession before the delighted gaze of the Sakchilli. When the last of the elephants had gone, the madman turned with a happy smile to his august master. "No! The diamond is not there. Perhaps the camels have it. Let the camels be brought out."

Once again pandemonium broke loose. Sages and philosophers came to assist their Royal Master in reasoning with the lunatic, but it was useless—it was the camels or nothing, and so the camels passed in regal state. And after the camels came, the cavalry and after the cavalry, the infantry and so on till even the servants and menials passed before the Royal dais, but still the diamond was not forthcoming. The Raja's face was purple. "Well!" he gasped, "You have seen all. Where is the diamond?"

The Sakchilli's face fell. Surely the "tamasha" was not over so soon? Were there not the poultry and the geese yet to be seen? And so, perforce, the royal chickens and geese passed by. And when the last bird had gone, a strange hush fell upon the watching multitude. It was the lull before the storm and the Sakchilli felt it and his knees began to knock. He looked at his august master and the Royal Eye was glassy. He looked at the multitude and they were licking their chops like wolves before the feast, and then he looked at the Syce and gave up all hope. He bowed his head in resignation and then all but died with joy and surprise for there, at his very feet, calmly seated below the dais, was the biggest and fattest of all the royal geese. With a scream he pounced upon the bird. "Here!" he cried, holding the bird up by the neck, "is the thief!"

In a moment the goose's neck had been slit, the diamond secured from its pouch and every one was patting the Sakchilli on the back. But the Raja was in a quandary. How could he give this madman a lakh of rupees? It is true the proclamation had been made, but the royal coffers were empty, and the August Presence paced up and down the dais, flipping his fingers in perplexity.

The Sakchilli watched him in amazement. What manner of man was this that cracked his bones without breaking them! After a while he timidly approached the King. "Protector of the Poor!" he enquired, "shew me this wonderful thing" and the Raja, more to gain time than satisfy a fool's curiosity, shewed him how to flip his fingers. At first the lunatic was unsuccessful, but once he had succeeded, the Sakchilli was overjoyed. Waiting for nothing more, he sprang from the dais, and rushed through the city shouting—"I have found the diamond. I have received the King's reward" —and then came nemesis.

Through the city the news flashed, and outside the city-gates, all the dacoits, rogues and thieves awaited the Sakchilli's coming. Down the road he came, dancing and singing and flipping his fingers, and suddenly they fell upon him in a body. But the Sakchilli had nothing to give. In vain they beat him and threatened to cut his throat if he did not reveal where he had hidden the money. It was useless, so as a last resource they flung him into the tank.

Wearily the Sakchilli swam ashore and lay down on the bank. After a while he thought of the King's reward and tried to flip his fingers, but with the wet and slime no sound would come. Distracted with grief he jumped to his feet rushing wildly round, shouting "I have lost it, I have lost it! The King's reward has fallen in the tank." Immediately, dacoits, rogues, thieves and lookers-on. stripped themselves to the waist; with one accord they rushed into the tank, and great were the feats of diving performed that day. But the Sakchilli lay moaning on the bank, and after a while the sun dried his hands and then, to his great joy, the King's Reward returned, but this time he did not let his neighbours know he had recovered it.

So to this day, in the city of Delhi, if any man receives a reward for which he has no use, his friends say—"He has received the King's reward," or if perchance he seeks something he cannot find, they whisper "He is diving for the King's reward."

CHAPTER XVI.

QUAINT TRIBAL AND RELIGIOUS CUSTOMS.

India provides some of the most extraordinary and fascinating instances of tribal and religious customs. To deal with the subject exhaustively would require a separate volume, I have consequently selected such instances, which from their bearing on the criminal activities of certain nomadic tribes will be most suitable for this book.

In recent years the police have been steadily tightening their control over the wandering tribes of India with the result that there is less danger from these classes than in the past. Of these the lambanies or gipsies are the most picturesque. In the days when the British troops depended on human beings for transport purposes, these people were very largely used, and they rendered splendid service. It is clear from the various accounts we have of them in old books that they were also carriers of salt, especially in the Deccan, where the British armies found them very helpful. The account of these wars is given by Briggs and he writes of the campaign in 1632: "The very first step which Mohabut Khan took in the Deccan was to present the Bunjaras (gipsies) of Hindustan with elephants, horses and cloths; and he collected (by these conciliatory measures) so many of them that he had one chief Bunjara at Agrah, another at Goojerat, and another above the Ghats, and established the advanced price of 10 seers per rupee (in his camp) to enable him to buy it cheaper."

Immense numbers of gipsies were employed by Wellesley in his Deccan campaigns for he believed that the commissariat was a most important part of his army duties. An early traveller in India, Barbosa, writing at the beginning of the sixteenth century says of this class, "They get up their cloths and shops at Cheul ..... they bring these in great caravans of domestic oxen, with packs like donkeys, and, on the top of these, long white sacks placed crosswise, in which they bring these goods; and one man drives 30 or 40 beasts before him."

The gipsies seem to talk a kind of patois which varies from place to place. In the Mysore State it is a mixed dialect called Kutni, largely composed of Mahratta and Hindi corruptions, and a mere knowledge of Kanarese will not enable one to follow their meaning. Many of them, of course, learn the language of the district in which they live. They have many curious customs, but they are most reticent about them. Dr. Short writes of this class in the Deccan: "Their social system is unique and they are guilded exclusively by their own laws and customs; that each community is governed by a priest, who exacts and receives implicit obedience, and who exercises, under the cloak of religion and supernatural agency, the undisputed power of life and death over them."

They maintain the closest secrecy regarding their customs and would sooner forfeit life than divulge them. Infanticide, human sacrifice, witchcraft and sorcery prevail among the different communities who can recognise each other by masonic signs. Witchcraft appears to be a strong power among them, and all kinds of disease are attributed to it. Solemn enquiries are still held in the wild jungles, where the Bunjaras camp out like gipsies, and many an unlucky hag has been strangled by the sentence of their secret tribunals.

They seldom have recourse to British courts in cases of trouble among themselves for the cases are usually decided by the priest or by the tribal council of elders. They are probably all guilty of many heinous offence against the law and they are all aware that, if one attempts to bring another before the court, their own deeds, would be revealed to the authorities. For, though these people are supposed to be engaged mainly as carriers, it is well known that they practise many unlawful methods. Dacoity is not uncommon; also cattle lifting, coining false money, and even the kidnapping of children. Whenever they appear in the neighbourhood, the people are on their guard, tor they know there is a danger of their possession being looted.

The introduction of railways and the development of roads all over the country have seriously affected the customs of these tribes, and the great Bunjarry caravans have almost disappeared, though occasionally one sees a small one in the country places. Carriers of salt and grain still follow the

A Bairaghi selecting his bride.

old methods. The grain is carried in shaped bags adapted to balance on the ox-pad and these carry about two hundred-weights of grain. When their journey is completed, which may be anything from ten to fifteen miles a day, the sacks are taken from the backs of the animals and are placed in lots, each family having a lot to take charge of. At daybreak next morning they rise and once more load their animals and continue the journey. The work of preparing the food is usually left to the women who accompany the caravan.

A large number of this class has now given up the roving life and have settled down in small villages. In Mysore these villages, which consist of rude wicker huts, are known as Thandas. In a few cases some of these tribes have built quite substantial houses and have settled down to agriculture. At certain periods of the year the members of the Labani castes meet at the jatras or festivals held in Mysore and the Deccan generally. It is a strange experience to see the greeting of these people who have probably not seen each other for a year—for they are very closely intermarried and so related to each in some direct or indirect way. They fall on each other's necks and weep for hours.

QUEER TRIBAL DANCES.

Tribal Dances in India are usually religious in character. They serve to illustrate some incident in the life of the presiding deity or are merely devotional. There is, however, a type of secular dances characteristic of a peculiar tribe or sect. It is these dances that provide some novel features and are typical instances of the extraordinary mentality of our primitive neighbours. It has been my good fortune to witness many of these quaint ceremonies, the more interesting of which I describe below.

THE MARRIAGE DANCE OF THE BAIRAGHIS.

Before describing the dance itself an account of how the Bairaghis select their wives will be interesting. The Bairaghis are a nomadic race indigenous to the districts round Purnea, Malda and Jalpaiguri. They are professional beggars and if the opportunity occurs professional thieves as well. Yearly they hold a great mela in the fields surrounding the ancient city of Gaur to which Bairaghis flock from all parts of the country. This mela is nothing more than a marriage market held principally to provide wives for the eligible bachelors of the tribe. The method used is a very simple one.

The parents or guardians who have marriageable daughters first state their desire to offer these girls in marriage. They then pay a small fee to the headman of the village who in turn announces on the morning of the first day of the mela the number of girls who are to be married and asks if there are any suitors for them.

The eligible bachelors, decked out in their gala attire, then present themselves and each in turn declares that he is willing to marry and able to support a wife. This ability consists principally in treating her with the scantiest courtesy, in forcing her to work to maintain him and his family and in demanding that she should dutifully love him and serve him all the days of her life. These preliminaries having been gone through, they each pay a sum of Rs. 2-8 and then retire to await the choosing ceremony which is held about midday.

The parents of the marriageable girls, meanwhile do every thing in their power to make the girls as attractive as possible. They are bathed and their bodies rubbed with oil and scented with uth and sandalwood paste. They are then covered with a single garment, made of white cloth, which completely covers their bodies and faces, so that no part is visible to the onlookers. They are then led into a large enclosure in the centre of the mela and made to sit in a row. At the appointed time the prospective bridegrooms arrive and enter the enclosure one at a time. Each in turn selects a girl and then retires with her to some secluded spot where she unveils or rather denudes herself of every strip of clothing, while her future owner carefully examines her teeth, her eyes and her limbs. No candidate for the Flying Corps goes through a more thorough examination than does this bride-to-be, for the Bairaghi husband is taking no chances. Sentiment never troubles him. His wife is a commercial asset, pure and simple, and as such he makes sure that he is getting a perfectly sound article.

If after the inspection he is satisfied, he says so and the fact is publicly announced by the headman of the village who declares them to be man and wife. If he is dissatisfied with his choice, he recovers her and leads her back to the enclosure, stating that he is dissatisfied and wishes to have another choice. He then pays another Rs. 2-8 and the process is repeated. If he is again dissatisfied he returns and pays yet another Rs. 2-8 but this time his selection, be what it may, is final.

After the choosing ceremony is over the crowd disperses but meets again that night when the marriage ceremony is celebrated. This consists in the most primitive of religious rites, such as the exchange of beads, garments, etc., the principal function being the consuming of vast quantities of arrack, toddy and cheap country spirits; accompanied with music, singing and the beating of tom-toms.

These preliminaries over the newly married couples retire to purpose for the more serious part of the ceremony—the Marriage Dance. It is impossible to describe this dance in detail—no self-respecting journal would publish this account if I did, but it has other characteristics which are interesting. The dance opens with a sort of "one-step." The women arrange themselves in a single line on one side of the square and the men on the other. To the accompaniment of drums they advance towards each other and retreat swaying from the hips and keeping time, the girls by beating their breasts and the men by slapping their thighs. During this part of the dance the humorous element is provided by scandal of the most brazen type. A "Buck" will shout out the name of his recently acquired wife proclaiming her to be a model of rectitude, of maidenly virtue and beauty. The "ladies" challenge this statement and some of the disclosures they make are positively startling. It is then the turn of the "brides." A sweet young thing will proclaim "her man" as a perfect Sir Galahad and then the bucks will give the interested audience an account of the secret sins of this unhappy youth that should be most disconcerting. But the extraordinary part is that every one enjoys this banter, including the victims, and I have a shrewd suspicion that these people glory more in their vices than in their virtues.

These dances usually conclude with a little humourous sketch. I have witnessed many such but will only attempt to describe the most decent.

When the dance is over, the whole tribe sit round in a circle. Into the open space in the centre steps a young man, with his wife and child. The child in this instance is a doll made up of straw with its head painted white. The young man then sings a song, proclaiming the virtue of his wife and the beautiful child she has borne him. When he has finished one or two of the audience approach the woman and ask to see the child. At first she refuses, pretending to be shy, but on their persisting produces the child timidly. The moment, however, she does so the entire audience raise a great shout of laughter and sing a refrain something after this style, "Its face is white and yours is black, How is this? How is this?" The husband then pretends to be furious and demands an explanation from his wife. Immediately she starts weeping and wailing and sings a number of impromptu verses describing her betrayal each ending with a chorus, sung by the whole tribe, "Bhaga topee wallah" (Away ran the European). This is a great favourite with the Bairaghis and as the women vie with each other in the lurid details of their infidelity, the moral effect on the audience must be disastrous.

THE RAIN DANCE OF THE RAJBANSIS.

The Rajbansis are another nomadic tribe who originally migrated from Sikkim and are now to be found all over the Terai. They are particularly remarkable for an extraordinary Rain Dance they hold during the period of droughts and famines. This dance is performed exclusively by women and it is considered most unlucky for any man to witness it.

I should like to describe one I witnessed in the Terai. It was amongst the Raibansis of Cooch Behar, the original inhabitants of these tracts, who have wandered north and spread themselves all over the Terai and Southern Dooars.

As even here these dances are extremely uncommon, I lost no opportunity to ascertain the exact time and place, and midnight found us (a local planter and myself) safely ensconced in a huge pepul tree, from which point of vantage we had a good view of the whole scene. What amused me at the very onset was the large number of men, boys, young men, old men and fossils of ninety summers and over, who, in spite of its reputed ill-luck, flocked to witness the performance

The dance was held in a small clearing in the jungle besides the half-dried bed of some stream. Shortly after we had taken up our positions about

The Rain Dance of the Rajbansis.

twenty women, mostly young girls, accompanied by some aged females bearing drums and cymbals appeared. In their midst they bore the image of some deity, whom I afterwards came to learn was called "Hudum Deo," a Rain God of great repute in these districts. The idol was made of mud and as far as I can remember was painted red. This they set in the centre and proceeded to watch the moon. This continued until the moon was fairly over-head, when the aged females started the music. The sound was not unpleasant, very much like the Mohorrum Drums punctuated at regular intervals by a sharp clang from the cymbals. The instant the music started the young girls sprang to their feet, they then proceeded to strip themselves nude and forming a circle round the idol commenced to dance, breaking the while into a wild plaintive chant. At first their movements were slow and certainly graceful and they seemed to be pleading with the god for some special favour—rain. But as the dance proceeded the music grew louder and more compelling. The movements of the dancers grew wilder and swifter and the plaintive character of their chant changed. Gradually they seemed to work themselves into a fury. Swinging their hands around their heads twisting and contorting their bodies, they whirled round and round. No longer did they plead with the god, instead they heaped every vituperation and abuse upon him—spitting and hissing at the idol. Their singing changed to songs of the most obscene type, till in a final burst of fury they fell upon the idol, breaking it to pieces and scattering the remnants in all directions. The music now ceased and the performers after dressing themselves returned to the village. All through this ceremony not a single male was visible, although I was perfectly aware and so probably were the dancers, that the whole population of the village were interested spectators.

The meaning of this dance is clear to anyone who has studied native customs. "Hudum Deo" the Rain God is worshipped all the year round by these people and so long as he does his duty and sends rain he is both venerated and loved. But the year he fails in this duty he is taken outside the village and disgraced in the manner described. Should rain fall during the dance, however, or the sky become overcast, the repentant god is brought home rejoicing and reinstated with every mark of respect.

A SHORT ACCOUNT OF THE TODAS.

On the rolling downs of the Nilgiri hills live an unusual people, unusual in appearance, unusual in customs, unusual in history. Indeed little is known of their history, and that little is mostly surmise. There are various theories as to their origin. The widest is that they originally came from Phoenicia. More likely is it that they migrated from Malabar or Coorg, in both of which countries are to be found points of similarity, either in customs or in racial characteristics. Their own explanation of their origin is amusing. When their great god On created the buffaloes, the sacred animals of the Todas, he caused them to come out of the earth, and hanging on to the tail of the last

The "Thi" or Conical Temple of the Todas.

(By courtesy of the "Times of India.")

buffalo was a man, who was the first Toda. And the god On then proceeded to take from the man a rib out of which he created the first Toda woman.

Originally they had their own gods, but gradually their worship has centred more and more round the buffalo, and now their religion consists chiefly of a mass of ritual and religious observance built up round the upkeep of the sacred dairies, and the care of the holy milk-givers Each family has its sacred buffaloes, and each village or "mund" has attached to it a sacred dairy which is looked after by specially ordained "priests."

Polyandry flourishes amongst the tribe. Generally several brothers have one wife, but women are also often passed on from one village to another. There is practically no crime amongst them, but they have their own village councils which spend most of their time in settling disputes concerning these matrimonial entanglements. Female infanticide is rife, though nowadays it is put down as much as possible. The unfortunate girl child used to be done to death by being trampled on by buffaloes. When a man dies one or more buffaloes must be sacrificed. The villagers drive a herd over the downs towards the relations of the deceased, and they have to overpower the intended victims by seizing their horns and bearing them down. As the animals are often infuriated by those driving them across to their doom, there is sometimes a great struggle, though there are seldom accidents. The victims are then driven into a kraal, and after some ceremonies and feasting they are clubbed to death.

The Toda does not believe in work. He tends his buffalo, and runs the dairy, and, strangely enough, does the cooking (which the women are not allowed to do), all manual labour is done by another tribe, the Badagas. The legend is told that the Badagas fled from Tippo Sultan in Mysore to avoid forcible conversion to Islam. They expected to find the Nilgiri plateau deserted, but to their consternation they were confronted by the long-haired Toda, who was, however, just as afraid of the unknown intruder as the newcomer was of him: so they struck a peaceable bargain. The Badaga agreed to work for the Toda if the Toda would give him land to live upon; and so it has remained.

The Toda women keep the houses clean, and do rough embroideries. As I have said, they are not allowed to cook, nor can they join in any of the rites connected with the care of the dairies. The "ghi" which is made from the milk of the ordinary buffalo is taken to Ootacamund, and sold at the weekly shandy.

To the ordinary visitor the Toda appears as a picturesque figure with his long black hair and beautiful almost perennial smile. The women are generally a distinct nuisance. If an unwary picknicking party settles down anywhere near a Toda Mund, the afternoon is made hideous by the cries of these females for "baksheesh." I dare say each unsuccessful bidder is beaten by all her husbands in turn after the hard-hearted foreigner has disappeared, and so they do their best—or worst. Their last resource is to sing, and they have doubtless learnt that the average easy-going visitor will hastily pay them to stop, so they do not often go away empty.

This puts one in mind of the tradition concerning the origin of a queer custom pertaining only to the hill tribes living in the neighbourhood of Naini Tal.

"WATER BABIES."

To the resident of Kasauli the "Water Baby" is no novelty. But to the occasional visitor, the sight of these infants lying peacefully by every brook and stream, while the water pours gently on their tender skulls, presents a pitiful if illuminating insight into the strange customs of the hill people who inhabit this part of the Himalayas.

As seen from the accompanying photographs, the *modus operandi* is quite simple. In order to ensure success the mother first blisters the child's scalp, at the crown of the head, with some vegetable caustic. She then selects a secluded spot besides a stream where she lays the child. With the assistance of a dried leaf, a split bamboo or some such contrivance, she diverts a portion of the water so that it falls in a thin continuous stream on the blistered portion of the child's head. The cool water acts as a counter-irritant, and the child, lulled to rest by the combined agency of this soothing treatment and the somniferous effect of some old-world lullaby, soon falls into a deep hypnotic sleep, from which it is awakened hours later on the return of its mother from her daily toil.

As to the origin of this custom, practically no

information can be gleaned from the people themselves. To all enquiries on this point they usually give a negative reply, and appear in addition suspicious and unwilling to discuss the subject with strangers. I was fortunate, however, in obtaining from an old resident of the district, the following narrative which is current among the natives respecting the origin of this custom. The tale is mythical, of course, and truly Indian in its conception.

Many years ago, in the days of their ancestors, there lived in this part of India a mighty king who had an only child,—a daughter. So beautiful was she and so good that the people called her Chand Bibi, because her face was as bright and as fair as the harvest moon at its full. The fame of her beauty spread to lands far and wide, and kings and princes sent costly presents to her father, seeking his daughter's hand in marriage. But to one and all alike Chand Bibi sent a curt refusal. Now it happened that Chand Bibi loved her cousin; but because of his poverty the King would not consent to her marriage and had her lover driven from the city. But when the moon was young the lovers met by stealth, as lovers will, and in the fullness of time a son was born. Then the King was furious and he had his daughter, her lover and child driven from the country, but after awhile fearing the child might grow up and wrest the Kingdom from him, he sent his soldiers with orders to kill the child and his father and to bring his daughter back.

In the meantime Chand Bibi, her husband and child, had taken refuge with the common people and worked daily in the fields, leaving their child in the charge of an old woman. One day news came that the soldiers were advancing, and every mother taking her child fled to the forests for safety; but because of the wailing of the children the soldiers easily found them, and every male child was put to death. But Chand Bibi had fled deeper into the woods and fearing that the wailing of her child should attract the soldiers to her, prayed to the Goddess Naini for help.

(To those unacquainted with the folk-lore of this part of India, it will be interesting to learn that the hill station at Naini Tal takes its name from the Tal or lake which is supposed to be the habitation of the Water Goddess, Naini, and it will be remembered that till quite recently, it was the custom for religious fanatics to cast themselves into this lake to propitiate the Goddess.)

Pitying the mother's distress and wishing to spare the child, the Goddess appeared to Chand Bibi and directed her to place the child on the ground. She then touched the hill-side and immediately a stream of water burst forth falling directly on the head of the child, lulling it to sleep.

Such is the traditional origin of this custom and to this day it is used by the Hill people for putting their children to sleep.

AMONG THE GONDS.

As I have dealt with one of our visitant gipsy tribes—the Bhairaghis, I feel that some mention should be made of another tribe, members of which, are constantly with us in the more dignified if less picturesque form of domestic servants.

It is a far cry from Calcutta to the Central Provinces, but many a master who proudly extols the sterling qualities of his "paharia" servant, is entertaining a "Gond" unawares. The "Gond" proper, born in the shadow of his sacred hill, Diwaligiri, is a "paharia" but not in the sense in which this term is understood by most people—as applied to the Nepalese or Bhutanese. The Gonds are "paharias" with the usual characteristics of this race. They are fearless, faithful, good domestic servants, born shikaris and usually honest. As to their antecedents, not being an anthropologist I can venture no opinion. To return, however, to a general account of the manners and customs of these interesting people.

The Gonds have a queer tradition regarding their origin. It appears that they were created near Mount Diwalagiri in the Himalayas, but their gluttonous and impure habits caused a foul odour to rise which offended the nostrils of Mahadeva, the presiding deity of this mountain. In order to be rid of them, Mahadeva, one day while bathing, created a squirrel out of a part of his body and sent it to run, with tail erect, before the Gonds. They thereupon, pursued the animal, following it into a cave which was the god's prison on earth. Mahadeva then quickly arose and taking a stone sixteen cubits long placed it before the entrance, placing also a giant to guard it. But four brothers had remained behind and these witnessing the imprisonment of the rest and fearing a similar fate, fled through the jungles, till they reached the "Kachikopa Lohargarth," i.e., "The Iron House in the Red

Hills." Here they found a giant who was first inclined to molest them, but as they put up a stout defence, he became pacified and gave them instead his four daughters in marriage. From this union sprang the present Gond race.

Of their history very little is known. They appear to have come, very much into prominence under Mahomedan rule in the 16th century. They then consisted of two distinct classes or sects, the Raj-Gonds or ruling section and the Dhur-Gonds or labouring class.

There is another clan of Gonds known as "Marias," a hill tribe found in the Feudatory State of Bastar. The " Maria " is a hunter pure and simple and it is these people who adopt the unusual method of lying flat on the back and using the feet to bend their powerful bows. In this attitude they have been known to drive an arrow almost through the body of a deer. The "Marias" are a wild, unsociable lot, living principally in grass huts, deeply suspicious of strangers and resenting interference of any kind. Once a year an officer collects their tribute for the Raja. This he does by beating a drum outside one of their villages and then absconding. The "Marias" then come out and deposit whatever they have to give in an appointed place.

Among the "Marias" there are two sects: The Bhils and Halbas. The latter make their living solely by distilling country liquor and worship a pantheon of deified distillers

The Gonds are a cheerful lot, dancing and singing whenever they have an opportunity. Their dances take the simplest forms. On moonlit nights the whole village will assemble in an open plot of ground and joining hands will circle round and round like children. When weary with dancing they sing impromptu songs. A man will step into the ring and sing a verse. He will be promptly followed by a woman, and as the song consists only in chaffing each other on physical defects, much merriment is caused among the audience.

Their religious ideas are of the most primitive type. The Gond pantheon consists of about fifteen deities, among whom "Thakur Deo" is held in the greatest reverence. He is the household god and presides over the home and the fields. Being omnipresent he has no particular image erected to his honour, but in the village of Jata, there still exists a few rusty links of an old chain which the Gonds affirm is the only form in which "Thakur Deo" has ever manifested himself. This chain is gifted with powers of locomotion and is occasionally to be found hanging from a branch, lying at the foot of a tree or in the bed of some old dried up stream, and on each of these occasions some humble offering is made to the god to the advantage of the attendant " Baiga " (priest).

Ghansyam Deo is next most widely known and worshipped. This god takes the form of a bamboo with a piece of coloured rag tied to one end. This bamboo is placed in a hut, specially constructed for the same, the floor of which is strewn with rough blocks of stone smeared with vermillion paint. Every November the villagers assemble to worship the god. On such occasions he is crowned with a garland of flowers and offerings of fowls and spirits

(Top) A mother placing her child near a stream.

(Below) Shewing the water falling on the Child's head.

are made. During the ceremony the god is supposed to descend upon the head of one of the worshippers, who forthwith staggers to and fro, seemingly bereft of his senses, till he rushes away into the woods. He is followed and recaptured by the young men of the tribe, who bring him back to the temple where he is exorcised by the priest. A scape-goat having thus been found, the year's misdeeds are now declared pardoned and the villagers return home rejoicing.

The "Baigas," also known as "Bhaimias," are the priests of the tribe. The office is hereditary, passing from father to son, and as these men are usually better educated and stronger physically, their supremacy is unquestioned. Besides his duties as a priest the "Baigai" is expected to take a leading part in all social and domestic functions. Some of their practices are queer. If a Gond falls a victim to a tiger, the "Baigai" is called. His duty in such cases is to appease the spirit of the deceased and to rob the tiger of the additional strength it has gained by killing a man.

THE TIGER DANCE OF THE GONDS.

The first and only occasion on which I had an opportunity of witnessing this curious ceremony was during a hunting excursion in the Feudatory State of Bastor. It was during a "beat" through a thickly wooded section of this country, that a tiger broke back, charged and killed one of the beaters and then made off.

Immediately it became known that a man had been killed the Marias refused to go on with the beat. In a body they collected round the victim and a runner was sent to the nearest village to summon a "Baiga" or priest. When this worthy arrived, he surveyed the body closely. Apparently satisfied he discussed the situation with the other Marias and then disappeared into the forest. For about ten minutes the beaters did nothing. They then opened out into single file and commenced beating the forest, just as if a tiger was in the immediate vicinity. This went on for some time, when, with a roar, the self same priest sprang out of a bush and rushed towards the beaters. At his appearance the Marias fled in every direction concealing themselves in the surrounding bushes. The Baiga now commenced an elaborate dance, emulating in a most realistic fashion the actions of a tiger about to spring on its prey. Round and round the corpse he circled roaring and snarling. Darting from one bush to another or springing swiftly across the intervening spaces, he gradually aproached the body till sufficiently near, when with a roar, he pounced upon it, taking up with his teeth a portion of the blood-stained soil. This was the final act in the drama. The beaters now clustered round the body and carried it off on a bier rudely fashioned with leaves and spears. I learned afterwards that this dance was necessary in order to free the spirit of the departed and rid the forest of the tiger. "Mai-Dharitoi"—Mother Earth is the chief goddess of the Baigas.

CHAPTER XVII.

HUMAN SACRIFICE & SLAVERY AMONG THE NAGAS.

As I am dealing with criminal tribes, I think a fitting conclusion to this book will be an authoritative account of the practice of Human Sacrifice and the existence of slavery amongst the Nagas, to this day.

The following account, culled from the "Statesman" of the 27th February 1925, and written by one of the party who accompanied Sir Harcourt Butler's expedition to the Nagas is so interesting and throws so much light on the peculiarities and customs of these primitive people that I have incorporated the extract, *in toto.*

" Of recent years the Hukawng (or Hukong) Valley has been chiefly heard of as providing a possible route for a railway to connect Burma with India.

From Ledo, on the Dibrugarh-Sadiya Railway, in Assam, to Sahmaw on the Mu Valley line of the Burma Railways, (a few stations South of Myitkyina), a line of less than 270 miles is required, of which about 60 miles would run through the Hukawng.

The Hukawng Valley is surrounded on the west, north and east by high hills. Those on the west form the boundary with Assam, those on the east form the watershed between the Irrawaddy and the Chindwin, while those on the north extend eventually to the Brahmaputra divide. These hills are sparsely inhabited by Singphos and Nagas.

The Nagas are a race who inhabit the hills of Manipur and the hills to the East and North-East of that State. In Manipur alone they number over 100,000. Slavery does not appear to be common among the Nagas, but head-hunting is a favourite occupation. T. C. Hodson in his book "The Naga Tribes of Manipur" writes:—

"The simplest and most obvious form of head-hunting is associated with the blood feud, where the duty of vengeance remains unseated until the tally of heads is numerically equal. Hence, as a matter of practical politics, it is usual when reconciling two villages to insist on the return of heads, for by this means a recrudescence of the teud is effectively prevented But there are other causes at work to account for head-hunting raids, which have their root deep in the religious beliefs of the people."

He described how a Chief's funeral is incomplete without the head of a human being, and suggests that the victim is killed by the community "as a solemn communal act in order that it may get some power over, remain in possession, as it were, of the great man who has been reft from them."

The practice of head-hunting prevails also among the Nagas in the Southern portion of the unadministered territory West of the Hukawng Valley.

In the Northern portion of that area, however,

the Nagas do not hunt for heads, but indulge in human sacrifice, the victims being either bought or kidnapped for the purpose. Most of the victims are apparently bought from the head-hunting Nagas and the price paid is about Rs. 500. For a fortnight before the date fixed for the sacrifice the victim is stupefied with drink, and then on the appointed day he is led to the top of the steps of the house of the person who is making the sacrifice, where his head is cut off.

The blood spurts down the steps and is considered to be an effective protection against bad spirits entering the house. The body is then cut up into bits, which are distributed and hung up in houses, at entrances to the village, at cross-roads or in the fields. The person who pays for the victim and holds the sacrifice keeps the skull (except for a bit of it which is given to the executioner) which he hangs up in his house. The object of the ceremony is to ward off sickness and secure good crops.

The Nagas, as already noted, keep slaves, and so do the few Shans of Maingwan.

The total area of unadministered territory which lies within the boundaries of the Province of Burma, and includes the Hukawng Valley and the surrounding hills is about 8,000 square miles of which the Hukawng Valley covers about 3,000. No estimate of the total population is possible, as most of the hills has never been visited by any European officer. Mr. W. A. Hertz, C. S. I., the Roos-Keppel of the North-East Frontier (now-retired) who visited the Valley in 1907, estimated the population of the Valley at about 16,000 of whom the Shans accounted for 425. He opined that the number of slaves possibly exceeded the number of free men. Many of the slaves he reported to be Assamese or of Assamese descent, while some of them were Kachins and Marus from the Myitkyina District.

In 1921-22 Lieut. Col. E. T. Rich, C. I. E., R. E., of the Survey of India, who was in charge of survey operations in this area, was asked to effect the liberation of any Indian slaves whom he came across. He found large numbers of half-breeds—descendants of Indian slaves and Singpho women—but only six Indians, of whom he was able to release three, the others not desiring to be released. Of these three, two had been kidnapped from Assam by Nagas and one had been sold to Nagas by fellow Indians.

It was in consequence of the information collected by Colonel Rich on the subject of human sacrifice among the Nagas, which attracted the attention of the authorities in Whitehall, that the Governor of Burma made his recent tour to the Hukawng Valley, the object of which was to impress upon the tribes the fact that the practices of human sacrifice and of slavery so close to the administrative border could no longer be tolerated.

Sir Harcourt Butler was accompanied by twelve officers, including Colonel Rich, the only officer now in Burma who has an intimate first-hand knowledge of the Hukawng Valley and the Naga Hills, and Mr. O. W. Tendrup of the Burma Frontier Service, a nephew of Mr. W. A. Hertz who has served for many years among the Kachins, and who made all the arrangements for the journey.

These arrangements included the making of a new road passable by motors for a distance of about 32 miles from an existing road to Shaduzup, the clearing of a mule-track from Shaduzup to Maingkwan, a distance of about 45 miles, and the erection of camps at Maingkwan and six other stages on the journey. The camps consisted of huts made of bamboo and grass, comfortable, if chilly, when it was fine, but somewhat cheerless when it rained. The party was accompanied by an escort of 100 Military Police under two British Officers.

We left Rangoon on January 16 and arrived at Mogaung on the morning of the 18th. There we detrained and proceeded by motor to our first camp. From there we proceeded on ponies by easy stages to Maingkwan which we reached on the 24th. As there was a heavy damp mist in the mornings which did not clear till 9 or 10 o'clock we generally did not start till 9 o'clock and we reached our destination well before lunch-time. The afternoons were devoted to sport.

According to Hertz and other authorities the country teems with game, big and small and the rivers with fish. It may be so, with the exception of doves and of snipes in the paddy fields of Maingkwan, the game kept itself well hidden, and the fish took no interest in the varieties of bait which were offered to them.

The jungle through which we travelled for most of the journey was of the evergreen variety and very dense. In places there were stately trees of enormous height of a species not recognised by any of our party. We did not see any teak or other timber of known commercial value. Round some of the villages were some large India-rubber trees. There used to be a flourishing trade in rubber, which was brought by Chinese traders, but the trade has now apparently died out. The jungle is full of leeches, who must have regarded those of our party who walked as a lucky and unexpected windfall.

On the 21st and 22nd we had a good deal of rain, and from Shaduzup to Maingkwan the track was in consequence very boggy in places and at times the ponies floundered in mud up to their hooks. On the 21st we crossed into unadministered territory, the boundary of which marked by nat (spirit) altars, such as one commonly finds at the entrance of a Kachin village, is the divide between the Irrawaddy and the Chindwin rivers. At the point where we crossed it, it is only about 1,200 feet above sea-level.

On the 22nd we arrived at Walawpum, the most important village in the Southern part of the valley. There, as elsewhere, the villagers lined up outside the village to receive us, placing their hands together as a mark of respect, in imitation, one supposes, of the Burmese shiko. The village "braves" fired off their matchlocks which make up for any lack of accuracy by great capacity for noise; the village band of gongs and clappers, played its little piece and the village burra-mems presented us with little posies of strange flowers. Some modification had to be made in this programme after the first day or two, because it considerably disturbed the dignified composure of His Excellency's Irish horse.

At Walawpum we had a long talk with the headman, Walawpum Gam, about conditions in his tract, and were given to understand (erroneously as it subsequently turned out) that under his enlightened rule there were very few slaves. Hertz described Walawpum Gam as a man of about 35 years of age with a benign countenance and a goatee beard, and as being an enlightened Kachin, with, however, the reputation of being a generous friend to the hired assassin. In 1915 he got into bad trouble in connexion with a Kachin rising, had his village burnt, and his slaves set free, and was deported for a term to Burma. He seems to have made a good recovery from the blow, because the village shows every sign of prosperity and he himself owns a couple of elephants. We saw, however, but few signs of his "benignity," and there was a distinctly forced air about his enthusiasm on all occasions when we met him.

On the 23rd we halted at Labawng. The headman of Labawng, Anai Tu, is a fat self-satisfied person who looked as though he was generally the worse for liquor. He is the chief owner of the hill on which the amber mines are situated.

We had no time to visit this hill as the road to it was reported to be very bad. The amber is dug out of the ground down shafts about two feet square or a little bigger, and some of these shafts are said to go down 60 feet, though they generally do not exceed 40 feet. These mines were visited in 1892 by Dr. Noetling of the Geological Survey of India, who reported that the fossil resin found there was very different from real amber so that the name Burmite was invented for it. It is produced in very large quantities but is mostly of very poor colour. The young men of the Valley wear rings and buttons made of it, and the women wear in their ears cylinders of amber shaped just like small carriage-candles. Rings may be bought for a rupee or two; the ear-cylinders for anything up to sixty rupees or so.

On our arrival at Maingkwan on the 24th we received a very warm welcome from a crowd of over fifteen hundred people, mostly Kachins, with some Nagas and Shans. Both Kachins and Nagas danced for our benefit.

A Kachin dance is performed by two long lines of people (mostly men, but there is no rule against women participating), who advance and recede side by side with short steps swaying to the sound of gong and drum. Each line has a leader, and the crowd follows the leaders with precision, and the path taken by the leaders is fixed by rules. A Naga dance is performed by a line of men who sway and hop slowly from side to side at the same time turning their dahs (knives) in their uplifted hands. The music is monotonous but not unpleasant, and has a somewhat hypnotic effect.

The warmth of our reception was no doubt in part due to the fact that the Government of Burma had invited all the chief headmen and other leading people from the valley and the adjoining hills to a big manao. A Kachin manao is a semi-religious dance and feast at which the participants gorge themselves on buffalo meat and rice and drink their fill of rice-spirit. At this particular manao over 30 buffaloes and a few mythun were slaughtered for food (a mythun is a cross between a bison and a domestic cow).

On the 25th His Excellency received the chief Kachin headmen and the question of slavery was discussed. The headmen seemed resigned to the fact that slavery would have to come to an end, and their chief concern was that the slaves when set free should not be induced to leave the villages where they now belong, and that slaves should not be given any inducement to run away at once before there was time to fix up the payment of compensation to their masters.

Certain Shans were then received, and complained somewhat bitterly that the Kachins took rice and buffaloes from them without payment. On the other hand, the Shans of Maingkwan own a large number of slaves and some very good paddy land. They would undoubtedly welcome British Administration, and, if protected against the Kachins, would soon become a very prosperous community.

Some Kachin headmen, who are over-lords of the Nagas, were next interviewed. They stated that the Kachins did not approve of human sacrifice but were unable to stop it. They undertook to prevent, so far as they could, any Kachins from the Valley being sold to the Nagas for sacrificial purpose.

Finally, representative Nagas were received, after they had been apprised by the Kachin overlords of the intention of the British Government to stop the practice. This interview afforded the most piquant moments of the trip.

The Nagas had two principal spokesmen; both were benevolent looking elders, and both with one accord, one with patient firmness and the other with a Zealot's fire, voiced the view of their tribe that it was inconceivable that they should abandon a practice, handed down to them by their fathers, and the stoppage of which would inevitably bring down upon them the wrath of the nats, causing their crops to wither, and themselves and their families to fall sick and die. Argument was in vain; but the interview served to impress upon them that stubborn as they might be in the one direction, they would find the British Government equally stubborn in the other.

Either on this or on the following day two slaves came to our camp and asked to be released. One was an Indian. He had been kidnapped 20 years previously from Assam by Nagas who had sold him to his Kachin master. He complained that for ten years he had to work in the amber-mines for his master and had got no wages, and that he was not even given clothes. He could hardly speak any Hindustani and, if released, did not propose to leave the Valley, but to settle down "on his own" at Maingkwan. His master claimed that he had bought him from the Nagas to save him from being sacrificed. After much haggling, he was redeemed for Rs. 100, which he agreed to repay to Government in four annual instalments.

The other case was that of an elderly woman whose son had run away into administered territory some ten years ago. He had now returned in our wake with Rs. 100 to buy his mother out. The old lady was eventually redeemed for Rs. 50.

On the 27th His Excellency held a Durbar. The site selected was a broad space between the two bamboo and grass buildings in which we lived. A bamboo dais was erected at one end, so that the site was enclosed on three sides. On either side of the dais facing the crowd two of our transport elephants were stationed. A passage was kept by the Military Police in the middle.

His Excellency and staff, all in full uniform, proceeded in the slow time customary at Durbars, the Military Police presenting arms, bugles blowing, and the elephants, disturbed no doubt by the bugles, trumpeting loudly. The crowd, who numbered over a thousand, squatted on the bare ground, some holding spears, some holding matchlocks, the Nagas in their red bamboo helmets, adorned with boars' tushes (and mostly with very little else on).

Sir Harcourt Butler opened the proceedings by saying a few words of welcome in Kachin, after which a Kachin official from the Myitkyina District read a Kachin translation of His Excellency's speech, announcing the steps which he had decided to take to put an end to slavery within the next three years, and the determination of Government to tolerate no longer the practice of human sacrifice, and warning the Kachins to cease molesting the Shans. This was listened to with rapt attention and low murmurs.

After the speech guns, silk skirts, serge coats, etc., were presented to the principal headmen, and cheroots and matches thrown to the crowd.[*] His Excellency then left the dais in procession, and the first Governor's Durbar in the Hukawng Valley was closed.

In the afternoon we all went down to the village of Maingkwan, about three quarters of a mile away, to watch the manao. More cheroots and matches and betel-boxes were distributed, and all the women got scissors, reels of cotton, needles and beads. This distribution took place while the various tribes performed their dances on the dancing floor. The floor was a circular site in the open, in the middle of which were erected a number of big posts painted with mystic signs, with a big drum suspended between two of the posts.

The dances were conducted with great verve, and one of the performers, whose heads and shoulders were covered with the beak and feathers of an enormous horn-bill, caused us much amusement by the coy way in which he clucked at us, with alcoholic solemnity, in supposed imitation of a horn-bill's cry.

Then one of our party gave a performance on a gramophone, which was much appreciated, after which we all adjourned to the fields between the village and our camp to witness a display of fireworks, which we had brought all the way from Rangoon. The fire-works were watched with breathless interest and were a fitting finale to what must have been quite one of the most interesting days in the memory of the oldest inhabitant of the Valley.

On the 28th we started on the return journey,

without any great regret, for the paddy fields of Maingkwan were a somewhat cold and damp resting place. The only incident of note on the journey occurred when we got to Walawpum on the 29th. Here in the evening the headman and his wife came to offer some presents to His Excellency with suitable expressions of loyalty, and were given presents in return and a cordial invitation to visit Rangoon next cold weather.

After these amenities the couple left the mess-hut, but within a very few minutes the headman's wife made a hasty and dramatic re-entry and casting herself on the floor wailed and sobbed and beat herself against the bamboo walling in a histrionic display of grief, which Sarah Bernhardt could hardly have excelled. Six or seven European officers were sitting in the hut reading the papers at the time, and the embarrassed stolidity with which they pretented to go on reading, as though nothing was happening, will be my most lasting memory .

When the lady had exhausted herself into coherence, we discovered that while she and her husband (who after the manner of husbands had discreetly made himself scarce) had been paying their ceremonial visit, two of her female slaves had run away to our camp to claim their freedom. And who, wailed Mrs. Walawpum Gam, would do the cooking, who pound the paddy, if these two were allowed to leave her at a moment's notice. The truant saving-maids were sent for, and their mistress reproached them bitterly. One maintained an impassive silence; the other sullenly answered back; she was not going to stop, it was a bad situation. She had with her a long string, on which she had made a knot every time she had had a beating.

If Mrs. Walawpum Gam had been a little less venomous in her bearings, some of us, mindful of the discomforts which inevitably follow when the cook packs her box suddenly and decides to leave, might have felt a certain sympathy for her. Eventually it was decided that the two women, could not be given back. A third slave-woman also came to our camp at Walawpum and found sanctuary. And when we crossed the divide into administered territory on the 31st, these three women crossed it with us, and by so doing automatically became free women.

From Walawpum our journey was uneventful. On the 3rd February we reached Mogaung and entrained for Rangoon, which we reached on the 5th.

It was a memorable journey. What its after-effects will be will depend on the decisions of the authorities at Delhi and in Whitehall. It is not likely to result in the immediate extension to the Hukawng Valley and the Naga Hills of the Montague-Chelmsford Reforms, but at least the "placid contentment of the masses" in those parts is likely to be rudely disturbed. The institution of slavery is doomed, and the substitution of free labour and consequent economic re-adjustment will be a lengthy and troublesome business, which, however, a liberal system of grants or advances will do much to facilitate. The stopage of human sacrifice is a far more complex problem, for here we are up against inveterate and deep-seated superstitions which all the riches in the world could not assuage, nor any fear of merely human authority and reprisals weaken. Now, however, that we know so much about the hideous cruelties attendant on the practice, there can be no turning back from the path already taken and eventually the Nagas will either have to confirm or perish.